Anonymous

The New-England Psalter, or, Psalms of David

With the proverbs of Solomon, and Christ's Sermon on the mount: being an introduction for the training up children in the reading of the Holy Scriptures

Anonymous

The New-England Psalter, or, Psalms of David
With the proverbs of Solomon, and Christ's Sermon on the mount: being an introduction for the training up children in the reading of the Holy Scriptures

ISBN/EAN: 9783337318307

Printed in Europe, USA, Canada, Australia, Japan

Cover: Foto ©Lupo / pixelio.de

More available books at **www.hansebooks.com**

The *New-England*
PSALTER:
OR,

PSALMS of *David*:

WITH
The PROVERBS of *Solomon*,

AND

CHRIST's SERMON on the Mount.

Being an Introduction for the training up Children in the *Reading* of The Holy SCRIPTURES.

BOSTON:

Printed by D. and J. KNEELAND, opposite the Probate-Office, in *Queen-Street*, for JOHN PERKINS, in *Union-Street*. 1764.

The Book of PSALMS

PSALM I.

BLESSED is the man that walketh not in the counsel of the ungodly, nor standeth in the way of sinners, nor sitteth in the seat of the scornful.

2 But his delight is in the law of the Lord, and in his law doth he meditate day and night.

3 And he shall be like a tree planted by the rivers of water, that bringeth forth his fruit in his season; his leaf also shall not wither, and whatsoever he doeth shall prosper.

4 The ungodly are not so; but are like the chaff which the wind driveth away.

5 Therefore the ungodly shall not stand in the judgment, nor sinners in the congregation of the righteous.

6 For the Lord knoweth the way of the righteous: but the way of the ungodly shall perish.

PSALM II.

WHY do the heathen rage, and the people imagine a vain thing?

2 The kings of the earth set themselves, and the rulers take counsel together against the Lord, and against his anointed, saying,

3 Let us break their bands asunder, and cast away their cords from us.

4 He that sitteth in the heavens shall laugh: the Lord shall have them in derision.

5 Then shall he speak unto them in his wrath, and vex them in his sore displeasure.

6 Yet have I set my king upon my holy hill of Zion.

7 I will declare the decree the Lord hath said unto me, Thou art my Son, this day have I begotten thee.

8 Ask of me and I shall give thee the heathen for thine inheritance, and the uttermost parts of the earth for thy possession.

9 Thou shalt break them with a rod of iron, thou shalt dash them in Pieces like a potter's vessel.

10 Be wise now, therefore O ye Kings: be instructed, ye judges of the earth.

11 Serve the Lord with fear and rejoice with trembling.

12 Kiss the son lest he be angry, and ye perish from the way, when his wrath is kindled but a little: blessed are all they that put their trust in him.

PSALM

PSALM III.

LORD how are they increased that trouble me? many are they that rise up against me.

2 Many there be which say of my Soul, There is no help for him in God. Selah.

3 But thou O Lord, art a shield for me; my glory, and the lifter-up of mine head.

4 I cried unto the Lord with my voice, and he heard me out of his holy hill. Selah.

5 I laid me down and slept; I awaked, for the Lord sustained me.

6 I will not be afraid of ten thousand of people, that have set themselves against me round about

7 Arise O Lord; save me O my God; for thou hast smitten all mine enemies upon the cheekbone: thou hast broken the teeth of the ungodly.

8 Salvation belongeth unto the Lord: thy blessing is upon thy people. Selah.

PSALM IV.

HEAR me when I call, O God of my righteousness: thou hast enlarged me when I was in distress: have mercy upon me, and hear my prayer,

2 O ye sons of men, how long will ye turn my glory into Shame? how long will ye love vanity, and seek after leasing? Selah.

3 But know that the Lord hath set apart him that is godly, for himself: the Lord will hear when I call unto him.

4 Stand in awe, and sin not: commune with your own heart upon your bed, and be still. Selah.

5 Offer the sacrifices of righteousness; and put your trust in the Lord.

6 There be many that say, Who will shew us any good? Lord, lift thou up the light of thy countenance upon us.

7 Thou hast put gladness in my heart, more than in the time that their corn and their wine increased.

8 I will both lay me down in peace and sleep; for thou, Lord only makest me dwell in safety.

PSALM V.

GIVE ear to my words, O Lord, consider my meditation.

2 Hearken unto the voice of my cry, my King, and my God: for unto thee will I pray.

3 My voice shalt thou hear in the morning, O Lord; in the morning will I direct my prayer unto thee, and will look up.

4 For thou art not a God that hath pleasure in wickedness: neither shall evil dwell with thee.

5 The foolish shall not stand in thy sight: thou hatest all workers of iniquity.

6 Thou shalt destroy them that speak leasing: the Lord will abhor the bloody and deceitful man.

7 But as for me, I will come into thy house in the multitude of thy mercy: and in thy fear will I worship toward thy holy temple.

8 Lead me, O Lord, in thy righteousness, because of mine enemies; make thy way strait before my face.

9 For there is no faithfulness in their mouth, their inward part is very wickedness; their throat is an open sepulchre, they flatter with their tongue.

10 Destroy thou them, O God; let them fall by their own counsels; cast them out in the multitude of their transgressions, for they have rebelled against thee.

11 But let all those that put their trust in thee, rejoyce: let them ever shout for joy: because thou defendest them: let them also that love thy name, be joyful in thee.

12 For thou, Lord, wilt bless the righteous, with favour wilt thou compass him, as with a shield.

PSALM VI.

O Lord, rebuke me not in thine anger, neither chasten me in thy hot displeasure.

2 Have mercy upon me, O Lord, for I am weak: O Lord, heal me, for my bones are vexed.

3 My soul is also sore vexed but thou, O Lord, how long.

4 Return, O Lord, deliver my soul: Oh save me for thy mercies sake.

5 For in death there is no remembrance of thee; in the grave who shall give thee thanks?

6 I am weary with my groaning, all the night make I my bed to swim: I water my couch with my tears.

7 Mine eye is consumed because of grief; it waxeth old because of all mine enemies.

8 Depart from me, all ye workers of iniquity; for the Lord hath heard the voice of my weeping.

9 The Lord hath heard my supplication; the Lord will receive my prayer.

10 Let all mine enemies be ashamed and sore vexed: let them return and be ashamed suddenly.

PSALM VII.

O Lord my God, in thee do I put my trust: save me from all them that persecute me, and deliver me.

2 Lest he tear my soul like a lion, renting it in pieces, while there is none to deliver.

3 O Lord my God, if I have done this; if there be iniquity in my hands:

4 If I have rewarded evil un-

him that was at peace with me: (yea, I have delivered him that without cause is mine enemy)

5 Let the enemy persecute my soul and take it, yea, let him tread down my life upon the earth, and lay mine honour in the dust. Selah.

6 Arise, O Lord, in thine anger, lift up thyself because of the rage of mine enemies: and awake for me to the judgment that thou hast commanded.

7 So shall the congregation of the people compass thee about: for their sakes therefore return thou on high.

8 the Lord shall judge the people: judge me, O Lord, according to my righteousness, and according to mine integrity that is in me.

9 O let the wickedness of the wicked come to an end, but establish the just: for the righteous God trieth the hearts and reins.

10 My defence is of God, which saveth the upright in heart.

11 God judgeth the righteous, and God is angry with the wicked every day.

12 If he turn not, he will whet his sword: he hath bent with iniquity, and hath conceived mischief, and brought forth falshood.

15 He made a pit and digged it, and is fallen into the ditch which he made.

16 His mischief shall return upon his own head, and his violent dealing shall come down upon his own pate.

17 I will praise the Lord according to his righteousness; and will sing praise to the name of the lord most high.

PSALM VIII.

O Lord our Lord, how excellent is thy name in all the earth! who hath set thy glory above the heavens.

2 Out of the mouth of babes and sucklings hast thou ordained strength, because of thine enemies, that thou mightest still the enemy and the avenger.

3 When I consider thy heavens, the work of thy fingers, the moon and the stars which thou hast ordained;

4 What is man, that thou art mindful of him? and the son of man, that thou visitest him?

5 For thou hast made him a little lower than the angels, and hast crowned him with glory

8 The fowl of the air, and the fish of the sea, and whatsoever passeth through the paths of the seas.

9 O Lord our Lord, how excellent is thy name in all the earth!

PSALM IX.

1 Will praise thee, O Lord, with my whole heart, I will shew forth all thy marvellous works.

2 I will be glad and rejoice in thee; I will sing praise to thy name, O thou most High.

3 When mine enemies are turned back, they shall fall and perish at thy presence.

4 For thou hast maintained my right and my cause, thou sattest in the throne judging right.

5 Thou hast rebuked the heathen, thou hast destroyed the wicked, thou hast put out their name for ever and ever.

6 O thou enemy, destructions are come to a perpetual end: and thou hast destroyed cities, their memorial is perished with them.

7 But the Lord shall endure for ever: he hath prepared his throne for judgment.

8 And he shall judge the world in righteousness, he shall minister judgment to the people in uprightness.

9 The Lord also will be a refuge for the oppressed, a refuge in times of trouble.

10 And they that know thy name will put their trust in thee: for thou, Lord, hast not forsaken them that seek thee.

11 Sing praises to the Lord which dwelleth in Zion: declare among the people his doings.

12 When he maketh inquisition for blood, he remembereth them: he forgetteth not the cry of the humble.

13 Have mercy upon me O Lord, consider my trouble which I suffer of them that hate me, thou that liftest me up from the gates of death:

14 That I may shew forth all thy praise in the gates of the daughters of Zion: I will rejoice in thy salvation.

15 The heathen are sunk down in the pit that they made: in the net which they hid is their own foot taken.

16 The Lord is known by the judgments which he executeth: the wicked is snared in the work of his own hands. Higgaion, Selah.

17 The wicked shall be turned into hell, and all the nations that forget God.

18 For the needy shall not alway be forgotten: the expectation of the poor shall not perish forever.

19 Arise, O Lord, let not man prevail, let the heathen be judged in thy sight.

20 Put them in fear, O

8 The NEW-ENGLAND PSALTER.

O Lord, that the nations may know themselves to be but men, Selah

PSALM X.

WHY standest thou afar off O Lord? why hidest thou thyself in times of Trouble?

2 The wicked in his pride doth persecute the poor: let them be taken in the devices that they have imagined.

3 For the wicked boasteth of his heart's desire, and blesseth the covetous, whom the Lord abhorreth

4 The wicked, through the Pride of his countenance, will not seek after God: God is not in all his thoughts.

5 His ways are always grievous; thy judgments are far above out of his sight: as for all his enemies, he puffeth at them.

6 He hath said in his heart, I shall not be moved: for I shall never be in adversity

7 His mouth is full of cursing, and deceit, and fraud: under his tongue is mischief and vanity.

8 He sitteth in the lurking Places of the villages: in the Secret places doth he murder the innocent: his eyes are privily set against the poor.

9 He lieth in wait secretly as a lion in his den: he lieth in wait to catch the poor: he doth catch the poor when he draweth him into his net.

10 He croucheth and humbleth himself, that the poor may fall by his strong ones.

11 He hath said in his heart, God hath forgotten: he hideth his face, he will never see it.

12 Arise O Lord, O God, lift up thine hand: forget not the humble.

13 Wherefore doth the wicked contemn God? he hath said in his heart, thou wilt not require it.

14 Thou hast seen it, for thou beholdest mischief and spite to requite it with thy hand the poor committeth himself unto thee. thou art the helper of the fatherless.

15 Break thou the arm of the wicked, and the evil man: seek out his wickedness till thou find none.

16 The Lord is King for ever and ever: the heathen are perished out of his land.

17 Lord, thou hast heard the desire of the humble: thou wilt prepare their heart, thou wilt cause thine ear to hear:

18 To judge the fatherless and oppressed, that the man of the earth may no more oppress.

PSALM XI.

IN the Lord put I my trust: how say ye to my soul, Flee as a bird to your mountain?

2 For lo, the wicked bend their bow, they make ready

their arrow upon a string: that they may privily shoot at the upright in heart.

3 If the foundation be destroyed, what can the righteous do?

4 The Lord is in his holy temple, the Lord's throne is in heaven: his eyes behold, his eye-lids try the children of men.

5 The Lord trieth the righteous: but the wicked, and him that loveth violence, his soul hateth.

6 Upon the wicked he shall rain snares, fire and brimstone, and an horrible tempest: this shall be the portion of their cup.

7 For the righteous Lord loveth righteousness, his countenance doth behold the upright.

PSALM XII.

HELP, Lord, for the godly man ceaseth: for the faithful fail from among the children of men.

2 They speak vanity every one with his neighbour: with flattering lips, and with a double heart do they speak.

3 The Lord shall cut off all flattering lips, and the tongue that speaketh proud things.

4 Who have said, With our tongue will we prevail, our lips are our own: who is lord over us?

5 For the oppression of the poor, for the sighing of the needy, Now will I arise (saith the Lord) I will set him in safety from him that puffeth at him.

6 The words of the Lord are pure words: as silver tried in a furnace of earth, purified seven times.

7 Thou shalt keep them, O Lord, thou shalt preserve them from this generation for ever.

8 The wicked walk on every side, when the vilest men are exalted.

PSALM XIII.

HOW long wilt thou forget me, O Lord, forever? how long will thou hide thy face from me.

2 How long shall I take counsel in my soul, having sorrow in my heart daily? how long shall mine enemy be exalted over me?

3 Consider, and hear me O Lord, my God: lighten mine eyes, lest I sleep the sleep of Death;

4 Lest mine enemy say, I have prevailed against him; and those that trouble me, rejoice when I am moved.

5 But I have trusted in thy mercy, my heart shall rejoice in thy salvation

6 I will sing unto the Lord, because he hath dealt bountifully with me.

PSALM XIV.

THE fool hath said in his Heart, There is a

God : they are corrupt, they have done abominable works, there is none that doeth good.

2 The Lord looked down from heaven upon the children of men ; to see if there were any that did understand and seek God.

3 They are all gone aside, they are altogether become filthy : there is none that doeth good, no not one.

4 Have all the workers of iniquity no knowledge ? who eat up my people as they eat bread, and call not upon the Lord.

5 There were they in great fear : for God is in the generation of the righteous.

6 You have shamed the counsel of the poor ; because the Lord is his refuge.

7 O that the salvation of Israel were come out of Zion ! when the Lord bringeth back the captivity of his People, Jacob shall rejoice, and Israel shall be glad.

PSALM XV.

LORD, who shall abide in thy tabernacle ? who shall dwell in thy holy hill ?

2 He that walketh uprightly, and worketh righteousness, and speaketh the truth in his heart

3 He that backbiteth not with his tongue, nor doeth evil to his neighbour, nor taketh up a reproach against his neighbour.

4 In whose eyes a vile person is contemned ; but honoureth them that fear the Lord : he that sweareth to his own hurt, and changeth not.

5 He that Putteth not out his money to usury nor taketh reward against the innocent. He that doeth these things, shall never be moved.

PSALM XVI

PReserve me, O God ; for in thee do I put my trust.

2 O my soul, thou hast said unto the Lord, Thou art my Lord : my goodness extendeth not to thee :

3 But to the saints that are in the earth, and to the excellent, in whom is all my delight.

4 Their sorrows shall be multiplied that hasten after another god : their drink-offerings of blood will I not offer nor take up their names into my lips.

5 The Lord is the portion of mine inheritance, and of my cup : thou maintainest my lot.

6 The lines are fallen unto me in pleasant places ; yea, I have a goodly heritage.

7 I will bless the Lord who hath given me counsel ; my reins also instruct me in the night seasons.

8 I have set the Lord alway before me : because he is at my

right hand, I shall not be moved.

9 Therefore my heart is glad, and my glory rejoiceth: my flesh also shall rest in hope.

10 For thou wilt not leave my soul in hell; neither wilt thou suffer thine holy One to see corruption.

11 Thou wilt shew me the path of life: in thy presence is fulness of joy; at thy right hand there are pleasure for evermore.

PSALM XVII.

HEAR the right O Lord, attend unto my cry, give ear unto my prayer that goeth not out of feigned lips.

2 Let my sentence come forth from thy presence: let thine eyes behold the things that are equal.

3 Thou hast proved mine heart, thou hast visited me in the night, thou hast tried me and shalt find nothing: I am purposed that my mouth shall not transgress.

4 Concerning the works of men, by the word of thy lips, I have kept me from the paths of the destroyer.

5 Hold up my goings in

7 Shew thy marvelous loving kindness, O thou that savest by thy right hand, them which put their trust in thee, from those that rise up against them.

8 Keep me as the apple of the eye: hide me under the shadow of thy wings.

9 From the wicked that oppress me, from my deadly enemies, who compass me about.

10 They are inclosed in their own fat: with their mouth they speak proudly.

11 They have now compassed us in our steps: they have set their eyes bowing down to the earth:

12 Like as a lion that is greedy of his prey, and as it were a young lion lurking in secret places.

13 Arise, O Lord, disappoint him cast him down: deliver my soul from the wicked, which is thy sword:

14 From men which are thy hand, O Lord, from men of the world, which have their portion in this life, and whose belly thou fillest with thy hid treasure: they are full of children, and leave the rest of

PSALM XVIII.

1 I Will love thee, O Lord my strength.

2 The Lord is my rock and my fortress, and my deliverer: my God my strength, in whom I will trust; my buckler, and the horn of my salvation, and my high tower.

3 I will call upon the Lord, who is worthy to be praised: so shall I be saved from mine enemies.

4 The sorrows of death compassed me, and the floods of ungodly men made me afraid.

5 The sorrows of hell compassed me about: the snares of death prevented me.

6 In my distress I called upon the Lord, and cried unto my God: he heard my voice out of his temple, and my cry came before him, even into his ears.

7 Then the earth shook and trembled; the foundations also of the hills moved, and were shaken, because he was wroth.

8 There went up a smoke out of his nostrils, and fire out of his mouth devoured: coals were kindled by it.

9 He bowed the heavens also and came down: and darkness was under his feet.

10 And he rode upon a cherub, and did fly: yea, he did fly upon the wings of the wind.

11 He made darkness his secret place: his pavillion round about him were dark waters, and thick clouds of the skies.

12 At the brightness that was before him, his thick clouds passed, hail-stones and coals of fire.

13 The Lord also thundered in the heavens, and the Highest gave his voice; hail-stones and coals of fire.

14 Yea, he sent out his arrows and scattered them; and he shot out lightenings and discomfited them.

15 Then the channels of waters were seen, and the foundations of the world were discovered: at thy rebuke, O Lord, at the blast of the breath of thy nostrils.

16 He sent from above, he took me, he drew me out of many waters.

17 He delivered me from my strong enemy, and from them which hated me: for they were too strong for me.

18 They prevented me in the day of my calamity: but the Lord was my stay.

19 He brought me forth also into a large place: he delivered me, because he delighted in me.

20 The Lord rewarded me according to my righteousness, according to the cleanness of my hands hath he recompensed me.

21 For I have kept the ways of the Lord, and have not wickedly departed from my God.

22 For all his judgments were before me, and I did not put away his statutes from me.

23 I was also upright before him: and I kept myself from mine iniquity.

24 Therefore hath the Lord recompensed me according to my righteousness, according to the cleanness of my hands in his eye-sight.

25 With the merciful thou wilt shew thyself merciful; with an upright man thou wilt shew thyself upright.

26 With the pure thou wilt shew thyself pure, and with the froward thou wilt shew thyself froward.

27 For thou wilt save the afflicted people: but wilt bring down high looks.

28 For thou wilt light my candle: the Lord my God will enlighten my darkness.

29 For by thee I have run through a troop: and by my God have I leaped over a wall.

30 As for God his way is perfect: the word of the Lord is tried: he is a buckler to all those that trust in him.

31 For who is God; save the Lord? or who is a rock, save our God?

32 It is God that girdeth me with strength, and maketh my way perfect.

33 He maketh my feet like hinds feet, and setteth me upon my high places.

34 He teacheth my hands to war, so that a bow of steel is broken by mine arms.

35 Thou hast also given me the shield of thy salvation: and thy right hand hath holden me up, and thy gentleness hath made me great.

36 Thou hast enlarged my steps under me; that my feet did not slip.

37 I have pursued mine enemies, and overtaken them: neither did I turn again till they were consumed.

38 I have wounded them that they were not able to rise: they are fallen under my feet.

39 For thou hast girded me with strength unto battle: thou hast subdued under me those that rose up against me.

40 Thou hast also given me the necks of mine enemies: that I might destroy them that hate me.

41 They cried, but there was none to save them: even unto the Lord, but he answered them not.

42 Then did I beat them as small as the dust before the wind: I did cast them out as the dirt in the streets.

43 Thou hast delivered me from the strivings of the peo-

ple: and thou haſt made me the head of the heathen: a people whom I have not known ſhall ſerve me.

44 As ſoon as they hear of me, they ſhall obey me: the ſtrangers ſhall ſubmit themſelves unto me.

45 The ſtrangers ſhall fade away, and be afraid out of their cloſe places,

46 The Lord liveth, and bleſſed be my rock: and let the God of my ſalvation be exalted.

47 It is God that avengeth me, and ſubdueth the people under me.

48 He delivereth me from mine enemies: yea, thou lifteſt me up above thoſe that riſe up againſt me: thou haſt delivered me from the violent man.

49 Therefore will I give thanks unto thee, O Lord, among the heathen; and ſing praiſes unto thy name.

50 Great deliverance giveth he to his king; and ſheweth mercy to his anointed, to David and to his ſeed for evermore

PSALM XIX.

THE heavens declare the glory of God, and the firmament ſheweth his handy work.

2 Day unto day uttereth ſpeech, and night, unto night ſheweth knowledge.

3 There is no ſpeech nor language where their voice is not heard.

4 Their line is gone out through all the earth, and their words to the end of the world; in them hath he ſet a tabernacle for the ſun.

5 Which is as a bridegroom coming out of his chamber, and rejoiceth as a ſtrong man to run a race.

6 His going forth is from the end of the heaven, and his circuit unto the ends of it: and there is nothing hid from the heat thereof.

7 The law of the Lord is perfect, converting the ſoul: the teſtimony of the Lord is ſure, making wiſe the ſimple.

8 The ſtatutes of the Lord are right, rejoicing the heart: the commandment of the Lord is pure, enlightening the eyes.

9 The fear of the Lord is clean, enduring forever: the judgments of the Lord are true and righteous altogether.

10 More to be deſired are they than gold, yea than much fine gold: ſweeter alſo than honey, and the honey-comb.

11 Moreover, by them is thy ſervant warned: and in keeping of them there is great reward.

12 Who can underſtand his errors? cleanſe thou me from ſecret faults.

13 Keep back thy ſervant

also from presumtuous sins, let them not have dominion over me; then shall I be upright, and I shall be innocent from the great transgression.

14. Let the words of my mouth, and the meditation of my heart be acceptable in thy sight, O Lord my strength and my redeemer.

PSALM XX.

THE Lord hear thee in the day of trouble, the name of the God of Jacob defend thee.

2 Send thee help from the sanctuary: and strengthen thee out of Zion.

3 Remember all thy offerings, and accept thy burnt sacrifice. Selah.

4 Grant thee according to thine own heart, and fulfil all thy counsel.

5 We will rejoice in thy salvation, and in the name of our God we will set up our banners: the Lord fulfil all thy petitions.

6 Now know I, that the Lord saveth his anointed: he will hear him from his holy heaven, with the saving strength of his right hand.

7 Some trust in chariots, and some in horses: but we will remember the name of the Lord our God.

8 They are brought down and fallen, but we are risen, and stand upright.

9 Save, Lord, let the King hear us when we call.

PSALM XXI.

THE King shall joy in thy strength, O Lord, and in thy salvation how greatly shall he rejoice!

2 Thou hast given him his heart's desire, and hast not withholden the request of his lips. Selah.

3 For thou preventest him with the blessings of goodness: thou settest a crown of pure gold on his head.

4 He asked life of thee, and thou gavest it him, even length of days for ever and ever.

5 His glory is great in thy salvation, honour and majesty hast thou laid upon him.

6 For thou hast made him most blessed for ever: thou hast made him exceeding glad with thy countenance.

7 For the king trusteth in the Lord, and through the mercy of the most High, he shall not be moved.

8 Thine hand shall find out all thine enemies; thy right hand shall find out those that hate thee.

9 Thou shalt make them as a fiery oven, in the time of thine anger: the Lord shall swallow them up in his wrath, and the fire shall devour them.

10 Their fruit shalt thou destroy from the earth, and
thier

their seed from among the children of men.

11 For they intended evil against thee: they imagined a mischievous device, which they are not able to perform.

12 Therefore shalt thou make them turn their back, when thou shalt make ready thine arrows upon thy strings, against the face of them.

13 Be thou exalted, Lord, in thine own strength: so will we sing and praise thy power.

PSALM XXII.

MY God, my God, why hast thou forsaken me? why art thou so far from helping me, and from the words of my roaring?

2 O my God, I cry in the day time, but thou hearest not; and in the night-season, and am not silent.

3 But thou art holy, O thou that inhabitest the praises of Israel.

4 Our fathers trusted in thee: they trusted, and thou didst deliver them.

5 They cried unto thee, and were delivered: they trusted in thee, and were not confounded.

6 But I am a worm, and no man; a reproach of men, and despised of the people.

7 All they that see me laugh me to scorn: they shoot out the lip, they shake the head, saying,

8 He trusted on the Lord that he would deliver him: let him deliver him seeing he delighted in him.

9 But thou art he that took me out of the womb; thou didst make me hope when I was upon my mother's breasts.

10 I was cast upon thee from the womb: thou art my God from my mother's belly.

11 Be not far from me, for trouble is near; for there is none to help.

12 Many bulls have compassed me; strong bulls of Bashan have beset me round.

13 They gaped upon me with their mouths, as a ravening and a roaring lion.

14 I am poured out like water, and all my bones are out of joint: my heart is like wax it has melted in the midst of my bowels.

15 My strength is dried up like a potsherd: and my tongue cleaveth to my jaws; and thou hast brought me into the dust of death.

16 For dogs have compassed me, the assembly of the wicked have inclosed me: they pierced my hands and my feet.

17 I may tell all my bones; they look and stare upon me.

18 They part my garments among them, and cast lots upon my vesture.

19 But be not thou far from me, O Lord: O my strength, haste thee to help me.

20 Deliver my soul from the sword: my darling from the power of the dog.

21 Save me from the lion's mouth: for thou haſt heard me from the horns of the unicorns.

22 I will declare thy name unto my brethren; in the midſt of the congregation will I praiſe thee.

23 Ye that fear the Lord, praiſe him; all ye the ſeed of Jacob, glorify him; and fear him, all ye the ſeed of Iſrael.

24 For he hath not deſpiſed nor abhorred the affliction of the afflicted: neither hath he hid his face from him, but when he cried unto him, he heard.

25 My praiſe ſhall be of thee in the great congregation: I will pay my vows before them that fear him.

26 The meek ſhall eat and be ſatisfied: they ſhall praiſe the lord that ſeek him; your heart ſhall live for ever.

27 All the ends of the world ſhall remember and turn unto the Lord: and all the kindreds of the nations ſhall worſhip before thee.

28 For the kingdom is the Lord's: and he is the governor among the nations.

29 All they that be fat upon earth, ſhall eat and worſhip: all they that go down to the duſt ſhall bow before him; and none can keep alive his own ſoul.

30 A ſeed ſhall ſerve him, it ſhall be accounted to the Lord for a generation.

31 They ſhall come, and ſhall declare his righteouſneſs unto a people that ſhall be born, that he hath done this.

PSALM XXIII.

THE Lord is my ſhepherd, I ſhall not want.

2 He maketh me to lie down in green paſtures: he leadeth me beſide the ſtill waters.

3 He reſtoreth my ſoul: he leadeth me in the paths of righteouſneſs for his name's ſake.

4 Yea, though I walk through the valley of the ſhadow of death, I will fear no evil: for thou art with me; thy rod and thy ſtaff they comfort me.

5 Thou prepareſt a table before me in the preſence of mine enemies: thou anointeſt my head with oil; my cup runneth over.

6 Surely goodneſs and mercy ſhall follow me all the days of my life: and I will dwell in the houſe of the Lord for ever.

PSALM XXIV.

THE earth is the Lord's, and the fulneſs thereof; the world and they that dwell therein.

B

2 For he hath founded it upon the seas, and established it upon the floods.

3 Who shall ascend into the hill of the Lord? and who shall stand in his holy place?

4 He that hath clean hands and a pure heart; who hath not lift up his soul unto vanity, nor sworn deceitfully.

5 He shall receive the blessing from the Lord, and righteousness from the God of his salvation.

6 This is the generation of them that seek him, that seek thy face, O Jacob. Selah.

7 Lift up your heads, O ye gates, and be ye lift up, ye everlasting doors, and the King of glory shall come in.

8 Who is this King of glory? the Lord strong and mighty, the Lord mighty in battle.

9 Lift up your heads, O ye gates, even lift them up, ye everlasting doors, and the King of glory shall come in.

10 Who is this King of glory? the Lord of hosts, He is the King of glory. Selah.

PSALM XXV.

UNTO thee, O Lord, do I lift up my soul.

2 O my God, I trust in thee, let me not be ashamed: let not my enemies triumph over me.

3 Yea, let none that wait on thee be ashamed; let them be ashamed which transgress without cause.

4 Shew m Lord; teach m

5 Lead me teach me: fo God of my salv do I wait all th

6 Remembe tender mercies ing kindnesses been ever of ol

7 Remembe of my youth, gressions: acc mercy rememb thy goodness f

8 Good an Lord: therefo sinners in the

9 The mee in judgment: will he teach h

10 All the Lord are merc such as keep h his testimonies

11 For thy Lord, pardon for it is great.

12 What feareth the Lo teach in the v choose.

13 His sou ease: and his the earth.

14 The se is with them and he will st venant.

15 Mine

wards the Lord: for he shall pluck my feet out of the net.

16 Turn thee unto me, and have mercy upon me: for I am desolate and afflicted.

17 The troubles of my heart are enlarged: O bring thou me out of my distresses.

18 Look upon mine affliction, and my pain, and forgive all my sins.

19 Consider mine enemies, for they are many, and they hate me with cruel hatred.

20 O keep my soul and deliver me: let me not be ashamed, for I put my trust in thee.

21 Let integrity and uprightness preserve me; for I wait on thee.

22 Redeem Israel, O God, out of all his troubles.

PSALM XXVI.

JUdge me, O Lord, for I have walked in mine integrity: I have trusted also in the Lord: therefore I shall not slide.

2 Examine me, O Lord, and prove me: try my reins and my heart.

3 For thy loving-kindness is before mine eyes: and I have walked in thy truth.

4 I have not sat with vain persons, neither will I go in with dissemblers.

5 I have hated the congregation of evil-doers: and will not sit with the wicked.

6 I will wash mine hands in innocency: so will I compass thine altar, O Lord.

7 That I may publish with the voice of thanksgiving, and tell of all thy wonderous works.

8 Lord, I have loved the habitation of thy house, and the place where thine honour dwelleth.

9 Gather not my soul with sinners, nor my life with bloody men:

10 In whose hands is mischief: and their right hand is full of bribes.

11 But as for me, I will walk in mine integrity: redeem me, and be merciful unto me.

12 My foot standeth in an even place: in the congregations will I bless the Lord.

PSALM XXVII.

THE Lord is my light, and my salvation, whom shall I fear? the Lord is the strength of my life, of whom shall I be afraid?

2 When the wicked, even mine enemies and my foes came upon me to eat up my flesh, they stumbled and fell.

3 Though an host should encamp against me, my heart shall not fear: though war should rise against me, in this will I be confident.

4 One thing have I desired of the Lord, that will I seek

after, that I may dwell in the house of the Lord, all the days of my life, to behold the beauty of the Lord, and to enquire in his temple.

5 For in the time of trouble he shall hide me in his pavilion: in the secret of his tabernacle shall he hide me; he shall set me up upon a rock.

6 And now shall mine head be lifted up above mine enemies round about me; therefore will I offer in his tabernacle sacrifices of joy; I will sing, yea, I will sing praises unto the Lord.

7 Hear, O Lord, when I cry with my voice: have mercy also upon me, and answer me.

8 When thou saidst, Seek ye my face; my heart said unto thee, Thy face, Lord, will I seek.

9 Hide not thy face far from me; put not thy servant away in anger: thou hast been my help; leave me not, neither forsake me, O God of my salvation.

10 When my father and my mother forsake me, then the Lord will take me up.

11 Teach me thy way, O Lord, and lead me in a plain path, because of mine enemies.

12 Deliver me not over unto the will of mine enemies: for false witnesses are risen up against me, and such as breathe out cruelty.

13 I had fainted unless I had believed to see the goodness of the Lord in the land of the living.

14 Wait on the Lord: be of good courage, and he shall strengthen thine heart: wait, I say, on the Lord.

PSALM XXVIII.

UNTO thee will I cry, O Lord my rock, be not silent to me: lest, if thou be silent to me, I become like them that go down into the pit.

2 Hear the voice of my supplications, when I cry unto thee: when I lift up my hands toward thy holy oracle.

3 Draw me not away with the wicked, and with the workers of iniquity; which speak peace to their neighbours, but mischief is in their hearts.

4 Give them according to their deeds, and according to the wickedness of their endeavours: give them after the work of their hands, render to them their desert.

5 Because they regard not the works of the Lord, nor the operation of his hands, he shall destroy them and not build them up.

6 Blessed be the Lord, because he hath heard the voice of my supplications.

7 The Lord is my strength and my shield, my heart trusted in him, and I am helped, therefore my heart greatly rejoiceth;

and with my song will I praise him.

8 The Lord is their strength, and he is the saving strength of his anointed.

9 Save thy people and bless thine inheritance, feed them also, and lift them up for ever.

PSALM XXIX.

GIVE unto the Lord, O ye mighty, give unto the Lord glory and strength.

2 Give unto the Lord the glory due unto his name; worship the Lord in the beauty of holiness.

3 The voice of the Lord is upon the waters: the God of glory thundereth; the Lord is upon many waters.

4 The voice of the Lord is powerful; the voice of the Lord is full of majesty.

5 The voice of the Lord breaketh the cedars; yea, the Lord breaketh the cedars of Lebanon.

6 He maketh them also to skip like a calf: Lebanon and Sirion like a young unicorn.

7 The voice of the Lord divideth the flames of fire.

8 The voice of the Lord shaketh the wilderness: the Lord shaketh the wilderness of Kadesh.

9 The voice of the Lord maketh the hinds to calve, and discovereth the forests: and in his temple doth every one speak of his glory.

10 The Lord sitteth upon the flood; yea, the Lord sitteth king for ever.

11 The Lord will give strength unto his people; the Lord will bless his people with peace.

PSALM XXX.

I Will extol thee, O Lord, for thou hast lifted me up and hast not made my foes to rejoice over me.

2 O Lord my God, I cried unto thee, and thou hast healed me.

3 O Lord thou hast brought up my soul from the grave: thou hast kept me alive, that I should not go down to the pit.

4 Sing unto the Lord, O ye saints of his, and give thanks at the remembrance of his holiness.

5 For his anger endureth but a moment; in his favour is life: weeping may endure for a night, but joy cometh in the morning.

6 And in my prosperity I said, I shall never be moved.

7 Lord, by thy favour thou hast made my mountain to stand strong; thou didst hide thy face, and I was troubled.

8 I cried to thee, O Lord; and unto the Lord I made supplication.

9 What profit is there in my blood, when I go down to the

pit? shall the dust praise thee? shall it declare thy truth?

10 Hear, O Lord, and have mercy upon me: Lord be thou my helper.

11 Thou hast turned for me my mourning into dancing; thou hast put off my sackcloth, and girded me with gladness.

12 To the end that my glory may sing praise to thee and not be silent: O Lord my God, I will give thanks unto thee for ever.

PSALM XXXI.

IN thee, O Lord, do I put my trust, let me never be ashamed: deliver me in thy righteousness.

2 Bow down thine ear to me, deliver me speedily: be thou my strong rock, for an house of defence to save me.

3 For thou art my rock and my fortress: therefore for thy name sake, lead me and guide me.

4 Pull me out of the net that they have laid privily for me: for thou art my strength.

5 Into thine hand I commit my spirit: thou hast redeemed me, O Lord God of truth.

6 I have hated them that regard lying vanities; but I trust in the Lord.

7 I will be glad and rejoice in thy mercy: for thou hast considered my trouble, thou hast known my soul in adversities.

8 And hast not shut me up into the hand of the enemy: thou hast set my feet in a large room.

9 Have mercy upon me, O Lord, for I am in trouble: mine eye is consumed with grief; yea, my soul and my belly.

10 For my life is spent with grief, and my years with sighing; my strength faileth, because of mine iniquity, and my bones are consumed.

11 I was a reproach among all mine enemies, but especially among my neighbours, and a fear to mine acquaintance: they that did see me without, fled from me.

12 I am forgotten as a dead man out of mind; I am like a broken vessel.

13 For I have heard the slander of many: fear was on every side, while they took counsel together against me, they devised to take away my life.

14 But I trusted in thee, O Lord; I said thou art my God.

15 My times are in thy hand; deliver me from the hand of mine enemies, and from them that persecute me.

16 Make thy face to shine upon thy servant; save me for thy mercies sake.

17 Let me not be ashamed, O Lord, for I have called upon thee:

thee: let the wicked be ashamed, and let them be silent in the grave.

18 Let the lying lips be put to silence, which speak grievous things proudly and contemptuously against the righteous.

19 O how great is thy goodness which thou hast laid up for them that fear thee; which thou hast wrought for them that trust in thee, before the sons of men.

20 Thou shalt hide them in the secret of thy presence from the pride of man, that shalt keep them secretly in a pavilion from the strife of tongues.

21 Blessed be the Lord; for he hath shewed me his marvellous kindness in a strong city.

22 For I said in my haste, I am cut off from before thine eyes; nevertheless thou heardest the voice of my supplications, when I cried unto thee.

23 O love the Lord all ye his saints: for the Lord preserveth the faithful, and plentifully rewardeth the proud doer.

24 Be of good courage, and he shall strengthen your heart all ye that hope in the Lord.

PSALM XXXII.

Blessed is he whose transgression is forgiven, whose sin is covered.

2 Blessed is the man unto whom the Lord imputeth not iniquity, and in whose spirit there is no guile.

3 When I kept silence my bones waxed old; through my roaring all the day long.

4 For day and night thy hand was heavy upon me: my moisture is turned into the drought of summer. Selah.

5 I acknowledged my sin unto thee, and mine iniquity have I not hid; I said I will confess my transgressions unto the Lord: and thou forgavest the iniquity of my sin. Selah.

6 For this shall every one that is godly, pray unto thee, in a time when thou mayst be found; surely in the floods of great waters, they shall not come nigh unto him.

7 Thou art my hiding place, thou shalt preserve me from trouble, thou shalt compass me about with songs of deliverance. Selah.

8 I will instruct thee and teach thee in the way which thou shalt go; I will guide thee with mine eye.

9 Be ye not as the horse, or as the mule, which have no understanding: whose mouth must be held in with bit and bridle, lest they come near unto thee.

10 Many sorrows shall be to the wicked; but he that trusteth in the Lord, mercy shall compass him about.

11 Be

11 Be glad in the Lord, and rejoice ye righteous; and shout for joy all ye that are upright in heart.

PSALM XXXIII.

REjoice in the Lord, O ye righteous, for praise is comely for the upright.

2 Praise the Lord with harp: sing unto him with the psaltery, and an instrument of ten strings.

3 Sing unto him a new song, play skilfully with a loud noise.

4 For the word of the Lord is right; and all his works are done in truth.

5 He loveth righteousness and judgment: the earth is full of the goodness of the Lord.

6 By the word of the Lord were the heavens made: and all the host of them by the breath of his mouth.

7 He gathered the waters of the sea together as an heap, he layeth up the depths in store-houses.

8 Let all the earth fear the Lord: let all the inhabitants of the world stand in awe of him.

9 For he spake and it was done, he commanded, and it stood fast.

10 The Lord bringeth the counsel of the heathen to nought: he maketh the devices of the people of none effect.

11 The counsel of the Lord standeth for ever, the thoughts of his heart to all generations.

12 Blessed is the nation whose God is the Lord: and the people whom he hath chosen for his own inheritance.

13 The Lord looketh from heaven: He beholdeth all the sons of men.

14 From the place of his habitation he looketh upon all the inhabitants of the earth.

15 He fashioneth their hearts alike; he considereth all their works.

16 There is no king saved by the multitude of an host: a mighty man is not delivered by much strength.

17 An horse is a vain thing for safety, neither shall he deliver any by his great strength.

18 Behold the eye of the Lord is upon them that fear him, upon them that hope in his mercy.

19 To deliver their soul from death, and to keep them alive in famine.

20 Our soul waiteth for the Lord, he is our help and our shield.

21 For our heart shall rejoice in him, because we have trusted in his holy name.

22 Let thy mercy, O Lord, be upon us; according as we hope in thee.

PSALM XXXIV.

I Will bless the Lord at all times; his praise shall continually be in my mouth.

2 My soul shall make her

d: the humble
f, and be glad.
the Lord with
exalt his name

e Lord and he
delivered me
rs.
red to him
ned, and their
hamed.
man cried, and
him; and ſav-
ll his troubles.
of the Lord
nd about them
and delivereth

d ſee that the
bleſſed is the
n in him.
Lord, ye his
is no want to
him.
g lions do lack,
ger, but they
Lord ſhall not
thing.
ye children,
ne, I will teach
the Lord.
nan is he that
d loveth many
ay ſee good.
tongue from
from ſpeaking

rom evil, and
peace and pur-

of the Lord are

upon the righteous; and his ears are open unto their cry.

16 The face of the Lord is againſt them that do evil, to cut off the remembrance of them from the earth.

17 The righteous cry, and the Lord heareth and delivereth them out of all their troubles.

18 The Lord is nigh unto them that are of a broken heart, and ſaveth ſuch as be of a contrite ſpirit.

19 Many are the afflictions of the righteous, but the Lord delivereth him out of them all.

20 He keepeth all his bones, not one of them is broken.

21 Evil ſhall ſlay the wicked: and they that hate the righteous, ſhall be deſolate.

22 The Lord redeemeth the ſoul of his ſervants: and none of them that truſt in him ſhall be deſolate.

PSALM XXXV.

PLead my cauſe, O Lord, with them that ſtrive with me: fight againſt them that fight againſt me.

2 Take hold of ſhield and buckler, and ſtand up for mine help.

3 Draw out alſo the ſpear, and ſtop the way againſt them that perſecute me: ſay unto my ſoul, I am thy ſalvation.

4 Let them be confounded and put to ſhame that ſeek after my ſoul: let them be turned

back

back and brought to confusion that devise my hurt.

5 Let them be as chaff before the wind: and let the angel of the Lord chase them.

6 Let their way be dark and slippery, and let the angel of the Lord persecute them.

7 For without cause have they hid for me their net in a pit, which without cause they have digged for my soul.

8 Let destruction come upon him at unawares, and let his net that he hath hid, catch himself: into that very destruction let him fall.

9 And my soul shall be joyful in the Lord: it shall rejoice in his salvation.

10 All my bones shall say, Lord, who is like unto thee? which deliverest the poor from him that is too strong for him, yea, the poor and the needy from him that spoileth him.

11 False witnesses did rise up: they laid to my charge things that I knew not.

12 They rewarded me evil for good, to the spoiling of my soul.

13 But as for me, when they were sick, my cloathing was sackcloth: I humbled my soul with fasting, and my prayer returned into mine own bosom.

14 I behaved myself as though he had been my friend or brother: I bowed down heavily, as one for his mother.

15 But in they rejoiced, themselves tog abjects gathere gether against it not; they d ceased not.

16 With hy ers in feasts, t on me with the

17 Lord, thou look on from their d darling from t

18 I will g in the great will praise the people.

19 Let not mine enemies joice over me: wink with th me without a

20 For t peace; but th ful matters a are quiet in th

21 Yea, th mouth wide said Aha, ah seen it.

22 This th Lord, keep Lord, be not

23 Stir up wake to my unto my cau my Lord.

24 Judge me, O Lord my God, according to thy righteousness, and let them not rejoice over me.

25 Let them not say in their hearts, Ah, so would we have it: let them not say, We have swallowed him up.

26 Let them be ashamed and brought to confusion together, that rejoice at mine hurt: let them be clothed with shame and dishonour, that magnify themselves against me.

27 Let them shout for joy and be glad that favour my righteous cause; yea, let them say continually, Let the Lord be magnified, which hath pleasure in the prosperity of his servant.

28 And my tongue shall speak of thy righteousness, and of thy praise all the day long.

PSALM XXXVI.

THE transgression of the wicked saith within my heart, That there is no fear of God before his eyes.

2 For he flattereth himself in his own eyes, until his iniquity be found to be hateful.

3 The words of his mouth are iniquity and deceit: he hath left off to be wise, and to do good.

4 He deviseth mischief upon his bed, he setteth himself in a way that is not good; he abhorreth not evil.

5 Thy mercy, O Lord, is in the heavens, and thy faithfulness reacheth unto the clouds.

6 Thy righteousness is like the great mountains, thy judgments are a great deep; O Lord, thou preservest man and beast.

7 How excellent is thy loving kindness, O God! therefore the children of men put their trust under the shadow of thy wings.

8 They shall be abundantly satisfied with the fatness of thy house: and thou shalt make them drink of the river of thy pleasures.

9 For with thee is the fountain of life: in thy light shall we see light.

10 O continue thy loving kindness unto them that know thee: and thy righteousness to the upright in heart.

11 Let not the foot of pride come against me, and let not the hand of the wicked remove me.

12 There are the workers of iniquity fallen: they are cast down and shall not be able to rise.

PSALM XXXVII.

FRet not thyself because of evil doers, neither be thou envious against the workers of iniquity.

2 For they shall soon be cut down like the grass, and whither as the green herb.

3 Trust

3 Trust in the Lord and do good, so shalt thou dwell in the land, and verily thou shalt be fed.

4 Delight thyself also in the Lord, and he shall give thee the desires of thine heart.

5 Commit thy way unto the Lord; trust also in him and he shall bring it to pass.

6 And he shall bring forth thy righteousness as the light, and thy judgment as the noon-day.

7 Rest in the Lord and wait patiently for him; fret not thyself because of him who prospereth in his way, because of the man who bringeth wicked devices to pass.

8 Cease from anger and forsake wrath; fret not thyself in any wise to do evil.

9 For evil-doers shall be cut off: but those that wait upon the Lord, they shall inherit the earth.

10 For yet a little while and the wicked shall not be: yea, thou shalt diligently consider his place, and it shall not be.

11 But the meek shall inherit the earth; and shall delight themselves in the abundance of peace.

12 The wicked plotteth against the just, and gnasheth upon him with his teeth.

13 The Lord shall laugh at him, for he seeth that his day is coming.

14 The wicked have drawn out the sword, and have bent their bow to cast down the poor and needy, and to slay such as be of upright conversation.

15 Their sword shall enter into their own heart, and their bow shall be broken.

16 A little that the righteous man hath, is better than the riches of many wicked.

17 For the arms of the wicked shall be broken: but the Lord upholdeth the righteous.

18 The Lord knoweth the days of the upright; and their inheritance shall be for ever.

19 They shall not be ashamed in the evil time: and in the days of famine they shall be satisfied.

20 But the wicked shall perish, and the enemies of the Lord shall be as the fat of lambs, they shall consume: into smoke shall they consume away.

21 The wicked borroweth and payeth not again: but the righteous sheweth mercy and giveth.

22 For such as be blessed of him shall inherit the earth, and they that be cursed of him shall be cut off.

23 The steps of a good man are ordered by the Lord, and he delighteth in his way.

24 Though he fall he shall not be utterly cast down: for the Lord upholdeth him with his hand.

25 I have been young and now am old, yet have I not seen the righteous forsaken, nor his seed begging bread.

26 He is ever merciful and lendeth: and his seed is blessed.

27 Depart from evil and do good; and dwell for evermore.

28 For the Lord loveth judgment, and forsaketh not his saints, they are preserved for ever: but the seed of the wicked shall be cut off.

29 The righteous shall inherit the land, and dwell therein for ever.

30 The mouth of the righteous speaketh wisdom, and his tongue talketh of judgment.

31 The law of his God is in his heart; none of his steps shall slide.

32 The wicked watcheth the righteous, and seeketh to slay him.

33 The Lord will not leave him in his hand, nor condemn him when he is judged.

34 Wait on the Lord and keep his way, and he shall exalt thee to inherit the land: when the wicked are cut off thou shalt see it.

35 I have seen the wicked in great power; and spreading himself like a green bay tree.

36 Yet he passed away, and lo, he was not, yea, I sought him, but he could not be found.

37 Mark the perfect man, and behold the upright: for the end of that man is peace.

38 But the transgressors shall be destroyed together; the end of the wicked shall be cut off.

39 But the salvation of the righteous is of the Lord, he is their strength in the time of trouble.

40 And the Lord shall help them and deliver them: he shall deliver them from the wicked, and save them because they trust in him.

PSALM XXXVIII.

O Lord, rebuke me not in thy wrath: neither chasten me in thy hot displeasure.

2 For thine arrows stick fast in me, and thy hand presseth me sore.

3 There is no soundness in my flesh, because of thine anger: neither is there any rest in my bones, because of my sin.

4 For mine iniquities are gone over mine head as an heavy burden; they are too heavy for me.

5 My wounds stink, and are corrupt, because of my foolishness.

6 I am troubled, I am bowed down greatly: I go mourning all the day long.

7 For my loins are filled with a loathsome disease; and there is no soundness in my flesh.

8 I am feeble and sore broken; I have roared by reason of the disquietness of my heart.

9 Lord, all my desire is before thee, and my groaning is not hid from thee.

10 My heart panteth, my strength faileth me: as for the light of mine eyes, it also is gone from me.

11 My lovers and my friends stand aloof from my sore, and my kinsmen stand afar off.

12 They also that seek after my life, lay snares for me, and they that seek my hurt, speak mischievous things, and imagine deceits all the day long.

13 But I, as a deaf man, heard not; and I was as a dumb man that openeth not his mouth.

14 Thus I was as a man that heareth not, and in whose mouth are no reproofs.

15 For in thee, O Lord, do I hope; thou wilt hear, O Lord my God.

16 For I said, Hear me, lest otherwise they should rejoice over me: when my foot slippeth, they magnify themselves against me.

17 For I am ready to halt, and my sorrow is continually before me.

18 For I will declare mine iniquity; I will be sorry for my sin.

19 But mine enemies are lively, and they are strong; and they that hate me wrongfully are multiplied.

20 They also that render evil for good, are mine adversaries, because I follow the thing that good is.

21 Forsake me not, O Lord; O my God, be not far from me.

22 Make haste to help me, O Lord my salvation.

PSALM XXXIX.

I Said, I will take heed to my ways, that I sin not with my tongue; I will keep my mouth with a bridle, while the wicked is before me.

2 I was dumb with silence, I held my peace even from good, and my sorrow was stirred.

3 My heart was hot within me, while I was musing the fire burned: then spake I with my tongue.

4 Lord, make me to know mine end, and the measure of my days, what it is, that I may know how frail I am.

5 Behold thou hast made my days as an hand breadth, and mine age is as nothing before thee; verily every man, at his best state is altogether vanity Selah.

6 Surely every man walketh in a vain shew: surely they are disquieted in vain; he heapeth up riches, and knoweth no who shall gather them.

7 And

respecteth not the proud, nor such as turn aside to lies.

5 Many, O Lord my God, are thy wonderful works which thou hast done, and thy thoughts which are to us ward: they cannot be reckoned up in order unto thee: if I would declare and speak of them, they are more than can be numbered.

6 Sacrifice and offering thou didst not desire, mine ears hast thou opened: burnt-offering and sin-offering hast thou not required.

7 Then said I, Lo, I come; in the volume of the book it is written of me;

8 I delight to do thy will, O my God; yea, thy law is within my heart.

9 I have preached righteousness in the great congregation; lo, I have not refrained my lips, O Lord, thou knowest.

10 I have not hid thy righteousness within my heart, I have declared thy faithfulness and thy salvation: I have not concealed thy loving kindness, and thy truth, from the great congregation.

11 Withold not thou thy tender mercies from me, O Lord: let thy loving kindness, and thy truth continually preserve me.

12 For innumerable evils have compassed me about, mine iniquities have taken hold upon me,

me, so that I am not able to look up: they are more than the hairs of mine head, therefore my heart faileth me.

13 Be pleased, O Lord, to deliver me; O Lord make haste to help me.

14 Let them be ashamed and confounded together that seek after my soul to destroy it: let them be driven backward, and put to shame that wish me evil.

15 Let them be desolate for a reward of their shame, that say unto me Aha, Aha.

16 Let all those that seek thee, rejoice and be glad in thee: let such as love thy salvation, say continually, The Lord be magnified.

17 But I am poor and needy, yet the Lord thinketh upon me: thou art my help and my deliverer, make no tarrying, O my God.

PSALM XLI.

Blessed is he that considereth the poor; the Lord will deliver him in time of trouble.

2 The Lord will preserve him, and keep him alive, and he shall be blessed upon the earth; and thou wilt not deliver him into the will of his enemies.

3 The Lord will strengthen him upon the bed of languishing, thou wilt make all his bed in his sickness.

4 I said, Lord be merciful unto me, heal my soul; for I have sinned against thee.

5 Mine enemies speak evil of me: when shall he die, and his name perish.

6 And if he come to see me, he speaketh vanity; his heart gathereth iniquity to itself, when he goeth abroad he telleth it.

7 All that hate me whisper together against me: against me do they devise my hurt.

8 An evil disease, say they, cleaveth fast unto him; and now that he lieth, he shall rise up no more.

9 Yea, mine own familiar friend, in whom I trusted, which did eat of my bread, hath lift up his heel against me.

10 But thou, O Lord, be merciful unto me, and raise me up, that I may requite them.

11 By this I know that thou favourest me, because mine enemy doth not triumph over me.

12 And as for me, thou upholdest me in mine integrity, and settest me before thy face for ever.

13 Blessed be the Lord God of Israel, from everlasting and to everlasting. Amen, and Amen.

PSALM XLII.

As the hart panteth after the water brooks, so panteth my soul after thee, O God.

2 My soul thirsteth for God, for the living God: when shall I come and appear before God?

thou in God, for I shall yet praise him, who is the health of my countenance, and my God.

PSALM XLIII.

JUdge me, O God, and plead my cause against an ungodly nation; O deliver me from the deceitful and unjust man.

2 For thou art the God of my strength, why dost thou cast me off? why go I mourning because of the oppression of the enemy?

3 O send out thy light and thy truth; let them lead me, let them bring me unto thy holy hill, and to thy tabernacles.

4 Then will I go unto the altar of God, unto God my exceeding joy: yea, upon the harp will I praise thee, O God my God.

5 Why art thou cast down, O my soul? and why art thou disquieted within me? hope in God, for I shall yet praise him, who is the health of my countenance, and my God.

PSALM XLIV.

WE have heard with our ears, O God, our fathers have told us, what work thou didst in their days, in the times of old.

2 How thou didst drive out the heathen with thy hand, and plantedst them; how thou didst afflict the people and cast them out.

3 For they got not the land in possession by their own sword,

neither

neither did their own arm save them: but thy right hand, and thine arm, and the light of thy countenance, becanse thou hadst a favour unto them.

4 Thou art my King, O God; command deliverances for Jacob.

5 Through thee will we push down our enemies; through thy name will we tread them under that rise up against us.

6 For I will not trust in my bow, neither shall my sword save me.

7 But thou hast saved us from our enemies, and hast put them to shame that hated us.

8 In God we boast all the day long, and praise thy name for ever. Selah.

9 But thou hast cast off and put us to shame; and goest not forth with our armies.

10 Thou makest us to turn back from the enemy; and they which hate us, spoil for themselves.

11 Thou hast given us like sheep appointed for meat, and hast scattered us among the heathen.

12 Thou sellest thy people for nought, and dost not increase thy wealth by their price.

13 Thou makest us a reproach to our neighbours, a scorn and a derision to them that are round about us.

14 Thou makest us a byword among the heathen: a shaking of the head among the people.

15 My confusion is continually before me, and the shame of my face hath covered me.

16 For the voice of him that reproacheth and blasphemeth; by reason of the enemy and avenger.

17 All this is come upon us, yet have we not forgotten thee: neither have we dealt falsely in thy convenant.

18 Our heart is not turned back, neither have our steps declined from thy way.

19 Though thou hast sore broken us in the place of dragons, and covered us with the shadow of death.

20 If we have forgotten the name of our God, or stretched out our hands to a strange God;

21 Shall not God search this out? for he knoweth the secrets of the heart.

22 Yea, for thy sake are we killed all the day long, we are counted as sheep for the slaughter.

23 Awake, why sleepest thou, O Lord? arise, cast us not off for ever.

24 Wherefore hidest thou thy face? and forgettest our affliction and our oppression?

25 For our soul is bowed down to the dust: our belly cleaveth unto the earth.

26 Arise for our help, and redeem us for thy mercies sake

PSALM XLV.

MY heart is inditing a good matter: I speak of the things which I have made touching the king: my tongue is the pen of a ready writer.

2 Thou art fairer than the children of men: grace is poured into thy lips: therefore God hath blessed thee for ever.

3 Gird thy sword upon thy thigh, O most mighty; with thy glory and thy majesty.

4 And in thy majesty ride prosperously, because of truth and meekness, and righteousness; and thy right hand shall teach thee terrible things.

5 Thine arrows are sharp in the heart of the king's enemies; whereby the people fall under thee.

6 Thy throne, O God, is for ever and ever; the sceptre of thy kingdom is a right sceptre.

7 Thou lovest righteousness and hatest wickedness; therefore God, thy God hath anointed thee with the oil of gladness above thy fellows.

8 All thy garments smell of myrrh and aloes and cassia, out of the ivory palaces, whereby they have made thee glad.

9 Kings daughters were among thy honourable women; upon thy right hand did stand the queen in gold of Ophir.

10 Hearken, O daughter, and consider, and incline thine ear: forget also thine own people, and thy father's house.

11 So shall the king greatly desire thy beauty; for he is thy lord, and worship thou him.

12 And the daughter of Tyre shall be there with a gift, even the rich, among the people, shall intreat thy favour.

13 The king's daughter is all glorious within; her cloathing is of wrought gold.

14 She shall be brought unto the king in raiment of needle-work: the virgins her companions that follow her shall be brought unto thee.

15 With gladness and rejoicing shall they be brought; they shall enter into the king's palace.

16 Instead of thy fathers shall be thy children, whom thou mayest make princes in all the earth.

17 I will make thy name to be remembered in all generations; therefore shall the people praise thee for ever and ever.

PSALM XLVI.

GOD is our refuge and strength, a very present help in trouble.

2 Therefore will not we fear though the earth be removed, and though the mountains be carried into the midst of the sea.

3 Though the waters thereof roar and be troubled, though the mountains shake with the swelling thereof. Selah.

4 There is a river, the streams

whereof shall make glad the city of God: the holy place of the tabernacles of the most high.

5 God is in the midst of her; she shall not be moved; God shall help her, and that right early.

6 The heathen raged, the kingdoms were moved: he uttered his voice, the earth melted.

7 The Lord of hosts is with us, the God of Jacob is our refuge. Selah.

8 Come, behold the works of the Lord, what desolations he hath made in the earth.

9 He maketh wars to cease unto the end of the earth, he breaketh the bow and cutteth the spear in sunder, he burneth the chariot in the fire.

10 Be still, and know that I am God: I will be exalted among the heathen, I will be exalted in the earth.

11 The Lord of hosts is with us, the God of Jacob is our refuge. Selah.

PSALM XLVII.

O Clap your hands all ye people, shout unto God with the voice of triumph.

2 For the Lord most high is terrible: he is a great king over all the earth.

3 He shall subdue the people under us, and the nations under our feet.

4 He shall chuse our inheritance for us, the excellency of Jacob whom he loved. Selah.

5 God is gone up with a shout; the Lord with the sound of a trumpet.

6 Sing praises to God, sing praises; sing praises unto our king, sing praises.

7 For God is the king of all the earth, sing ye praises with understanding.

8 God reigneth over the heathen; God sitteth upon the throne of his holiness.

9 The princes of the people are gathered together, even the people of the God of Abraham: for the shields of the earth belong unto God; he is greatly exalted.

PSALM XLVIII.

GReat is the Lord, and greatly to be praised in the city of our God, in the mountain of his holiness.

2 Beautiful for situation, the joy of the whole earth is mount Zion on the sides of the north, the city of the great king.

3 God is known in her palaces for a refuge.

4 For, lo, the kings were assembled, they passed by together.

5 They saw it, and so they marvelled, they were troubled, and hasted away.

6 Fear took hold upon them there, and pain, as of a woman in travail.

7 Thou breakest the ships

iniquity of my heels shall compass me about.

6 They that trust in their wealth, and boast themselves in the multitude of their riches:

7 None of them can by any means redeem his brother, nor give to God a ransom for him.

8 (For the redemption of their soul is precious, and it ceaseth for ever.)

9 That he should still live for ever, and not see corruption.

10 For he seeth that wise men die, likewise the fool, and the brutish person perish, and leave their wealth to others.

11 Their inward thought is, that their houses shall continue for ever, and their dwelling-places to all generations; they call their lands after their own names.

12 Nevertheless, man being in honour abideth not; he is like the beasts that perish.

13 This their way is their folly, yet their posterity approve their sayings. Selah.

14 Like sheep they are laid in the grave, death shall feed on them: and the upright shall have dominion over them in the morning, and their beauty shall consume in the grave, from their dwelling.

15 But god will redeem my soul from the power of the grave; for he shall receive me. Selah.

16 Be not thou afraid when

one is made rich, when the glory of his house is increased.

17 For when he dieth he shall carry nothing away : his glory shall not descend after him.

18 Though whiles he lived, he blessed his soul : and men will praise thee when thou doest well to thyself.

19 He shall go to the generation of his fathers, they shall never see light.

20 Man that is in honour and understandeth not, is like the beasts that perish.

PSALM L.

THE mighty God, even the Lord hath spoken, and called the earth from the rising of the sun, unto the going down thereof.

2 Out of Zion, the perfection of beauty, God hath shined.

3 Our God shall come, and shall not keep silence : a fire shall devour before him, and it shall be very tempestuous round about him.

4 He shall call to the heavens from above, and to the earth, that he may judge his people.

5 Gather my saints together unto me : those that have made a covenant with me by sacrifice.

6 And the heavens shall de-

8 I will not thy sacrifices, offerings, to tinually before

9 I will tak of thy house, of thy folds.

10 For eve forest is mine upon a thousa

11 I know the mountains beasts of the fie

12 If I were not tell thee : mine, and the

13 Will I bulls, or drin goats ?

14 Offer u giving, and pa the Most Hig

15 And cal day of trouble thee, and thou

16 But u God saith, W do to declare that thou sho covenant in th

17 Seeing struction, and behind thee.

18 When thief, then

against thy brother; thou slanderest thine own mother's son.

21 These things hast thou done, and I kept silence: thou thoughtest that I was altogether such a one as thyself: but I will reprove thee, and set them in order before thine eyes.

22 Now consider this, ye that forget God, lest I tear you in pieces, and there be none to deliver.

23 Whoso offereth praise, glorifieth me: and to him that ordereth his conversation aright, will I shew the salvation of God.

PSALM LI.

Have mercy upon me, O God, according to thy loving kindness: according unto the multitude of thy tender mercies, blot out my transgressions.

2 Wash me throughly from mine iniquity, and cleanse me from my sin.

3 For I acknowledge my transgressions: and my sin is ever before me.

4 Against thee, thee only have I sinned, and done this evil in thy sight: that thou mightest be justified when thou speakest, and be clear when thou judgest.

5 Behold, I was shapen in iniquity: and in sin did my mother conceive me.

6 Behold, thou desirest truth in the inward parts: and in the hidden part thou shalt make me to know wisdom.

7 Purge me with hyssop, and I shall be clean: wash me, and I shall be whiter than snow.

8 Make me to hear joy and gladness: that the bones which thou hast broken, may rejoice.

9 Hide thy face from my sins, and blot out all mine iniquities.

10 Create in me a clean heart, O God? and renew a right spirit within me.

11 Cast me not away from thy presence; and take not thy holy spirit from me.

12 Restore unto me the joy of thy salvation: and uphold me with thy free spirit.

13 Then will I teach transgressors thy ways, and sinners shall be converted unto thee.

14 Deliver me from blood-guiltiness, O God, thou God of my salvation: & my tongue shall sing aloud of thy righteousness.

15 O Lord, open thou my lips, and my mouth shall shew forth thy praise,

16 For thou desirest not sacrifice, else would I give it: thou delightest not in burnt-offering.

17 The sacrifices of God are a broken spirit: a broken and a contrite heart, O God, thou wilt not despise.

18 Do good in thy good pleasure unto Zion: build thou the walls of Jerusalem.

19 Then shalt thou be pleased with the sacrifices of righteousness, with burnt-offering and whole-burnt-offer-

ing: then shall they offer bullocks upon thine altar.

PSALM LII.

WHY boastest thou thyself in mischief, O mighty man? the goodness of God endureth continually.

2 Thy tongue deviseth mischiefs: like a sharp razor, working deceitfully.

3 Thou lovest evil more than good: and lying rather than to speak righteousness. Selah.

4 Thou lovest all devouring words, O thou deceitful tongue.

5 God shall likewise destroy thee for ever, he shall take thee away, and pluck thee out of thy dwelling-place, & root thee out of the land of the living. Selah.

6 The righteous also shall see and fear, and shall laugh at him.

7 Lo, this is the man that made not God his strength: but trusted in the abundance of his riches, and strengthened himself in his wickedness.

8 But I am like a green olive tree in the house of God: I trust in the mercy of God for ever and ever.

9 I will praise thee for ever, because thou haste done it: and I will wait on thy name, for it is good before thy saints.

PSALM LIII.

THE fool hath said in his heart, There is no God; corrupt are they, and have done abominable iniquity: there is none that doth good.

2 God looked down from heaven upon the children of men, to see if there were any that did understand, that did seek God.

3 Every one of them is gone back, they are altogether become filthy; there is none that doeth good, no not one.

4 Have the workers of iniquity no knowledge? who eat up my people, as they eat bread; they have not called upon God.

5 There were they in great fear, where no fear was: for God hath scattered the bones of him that encampeth against thee, thou hast put them to shame, because God hath despised them.

6 O that the salvation of Israel were come out of Zion! when God bringeth back the captivity of his people, Jacob shall rejoice, and Israel shall be glad.

PSALM LIV.

SAVE me, O God, by thy Name, and judge me by thy strength.

2 Hear my prayer, O God; give ear to the words of my mouth.

3 For strangers are risen up against me, and oppressors seek after my soul; they have not set God before them. Selah.

4 Behold, God is mine helper: the Lord is with them that uphold my soul.

5 He shall reward evil unto mine enemies; cut them off in

thy truth.

6 I will freely sacrifice unto thee; I will praise thy Name, O Lord, for it is good.

7 For he hath delivered me out of all trouble: and mine eye hath seen his desire upon mine enemies.

PSALM LV.

GIVE ear to my prayer, O God: and hide not thyself from my supplication.

2 Attend unto me and hear me: I mourn in my complaint, and make a noise,

3 Because of the voice of the enemy, because of the oppression of the wicked: for they cast iniquity upon me, and in wrath they hate me.

4 My heart is sore pained within me: and the terrors of death are fallen upon me.

5 Fearfulness and trembling are come upon me, and horror hath overwhelmed me.

6 And I said, O that I had wings like a dove! for then would I fly away and be at rest.

7 Lo then would I wander far off, and remain in the wilderness. Selah.

8 I would hasten my escape from the windy storm and tempest.

9 Destroy, O Lord and divide their tongues: for I have seen violence and strife in the city.

10 Day and night they go about it upon the walls thereof: mischief also and sorrow are in the midst of it.

11 Wickedness is in the midst thereof: deceit and guile depart not from her streets.

12 For it was an enemy that reproached me, then I could have borne it; neither was it he that hated me, that did magnify himself against me, then I would have hid myself from him.

13 But it was thou, a man, mine equal, my guide, and mine acquaintance.

14 We took sweet counsel together, and walked unto the house of God in company.

15 Let death seize upon them, and let them go down quick into hell: for wickedness is in their dwellings, and among them.

16 As for me, I will call upon God: and the Lord shall save me.

17 Evening and morning, and at noon will I pray, and cry aloud: and he shall hear my voice.

18 He hath delivered my soul in peace from the battle that was against me, for there were many with me.

19 God shall hear and afflict them, even he that abideth of old, Selah: because they have no changes, therefore they fear not God.

20 He hath put forth his hands against such as be at peace with him: he hath bro-

ken his covenant.

21 The words of his mouth were smoother than butter, but war was in his heart: his words were softer than oil, yet were they drawn swords.

22 Cast thy burden upon the Lord, and he shall sustain thee: he shall never suffer the righteous to be moved.

23 But thou, O God, shalt bring them down into the pit of destruction: bloody and deceitful men shall not live out half their days, but I will trust in thee.

PSALM LVI.

BE merciful unto me, O God, for man would swallow me up: he fighting daily oppresseth me.

2 Mine enemies would daily swallow me up: For they be many that fight against me, O thou most High.

3 What time I am afraid, I will trust in thee.

4 In God I will praise his word, in God I have put my trust, I will not fear what flesh can do unto me.

5 Every day they wrest my words: all their thoughts are against me for evil.

6 They gather themselves

8 Thou tellest my wanderings, put thou my tears into thy bottle: are they not in thy book?

9 When I cry unto thee, then shall mine enemies turn back: this I know, for God is for me.

10 In God will I praise his word: in the Lord will I praise his word.

11 In God have I put my trust: I will not be afraid what man can do unto me.

12 Thy vows are upon me, O God: I will render praises unto thee.

13 For thou hast delivered my soul from death: wilt not thou deliver my feet from falling, that I may walk before God in the light of the living?

PSALM LVII.

BE merciful unto me, O God, be merciful unto me, for my soul trusteth in thee: yea, in the shadow of thy wings will I make my refuge, until these calamities be overpast.

2 I will cry unto God most high: unto God that performeth all things for me.

3 He shall send from heaven, and save me from the reproach of him that would swallow me

and arrows, and their tongue a sharp sword.

5 Be thou exalted, O God above the heavens, let thy glory be above all the Earth

6 They have prepared a net for my steps, my soul is bowed down: they have digged a pit before me, into the midst whereof they are fallen themselves. Selah.

7 My heart is fixed, O God, my heart is fixed; I will sing and give praise.

8 Awake up, my glory, awake, psaltery and harp: I myself will awake early.

9 I will praise thee, O Lord, among the people: I will sing unto thee among the nations.

10 For thy mercy is great unto the heavens, and thy truth unto the clouds.

11 Be thou exalted, O God above the heavens: let thy glory be above all the earth.

PSALM LVIII.

DO ye indeed speak righteousness, O congregation? do ye judge uprightly, ye sons of men?

2 Yea, in heart you work wickedness, you weigh the violence of your hands in the earth

3 The wicked are estranged from the womb: they go astray as soon as they be born, speaking lies.

4 Their poison is like the poison of a serpent; they are like the deaf adder, that stoppeth her ear.

5 Which will not hearken to the voice of charmers, charming never so wisely.

6 Break their teeth, O God, in their mouth: break out the great teeth of the young lions, O Lord.

7 Let them melt away as waters, which run continually; when he bendeth his bow to shoot his arrows, let them be as cut in pieces,

8 As a snail which melteth, let every one of them pass away; like the untimely birth of a woman, that they may not see the sun.

9 Before your pots can feel the thorns, he shall take them away, as with a whirlwind, both living and in his wrath.

10 The righteous shall rejoice when he seeth the vengeance: he shall wash his feet in the blood of the wicked.

11 So that a man shall say, Verily there is a reward for the righteous: verily he is a God that judgeth in the earth.

PSALM LIX.

DEliver me from mine enemines, O my God: defend me from them that rise up against me.

2 Deliver me from the workers of iniquity, and save me from bloody men.

3 For lo, they lie in wait for my soul: the mighty are gathered aginst me; not for my

transgression, nor for my sin, O Lord.

4 They run and prepare themselves without my fault awake to help me, and behold.

5 Thou therefore, O Lord God of hosts, the God of Israel, awake to visit all the heathen: be not merciful to any wicked transgressors. Selah.

6 They return at evening: they make a noise like a dog, and go round about the city.

7 Behold they belch out with their mouth: swords are in their lips; for who (say they) doth hear?

8 But thou, O Lord, shalt laugh at them; thou shalt have all the heathen in derision.

9 Because of his strength will I wait upon thee: for God is my defence.

10 The God of my mercy shall prevent me: God shall let me see my desire upon mine enemies.

11 Slay them not, lest my people forget: scatter them by thy power; and bring them down, O Lord our shield.

12 For the sin of their mouth and the words of their lips, let them even be taken in their pride: and for cursing and lying which they speak.

13 Consume them in wrath, consume them, that they may not be: and let them know that God ruleth in Jacob, unto the ends of the earth. Selah.

14 And at e return, and le noise like a dog about the city.

15 Let them down for meat they be not sat

16 But I will er; yea, I will mercy in the m hast been my de in the day of

17 Unto strength, will is my defence, my mercy.

PSAL

O God, th off, the us, thou hast O turn thyself

2 Thou has to tremble; th it: heal the for it shaketh.

3 Thou ha people hard th made us to d astonishment.

4 Thou ha to them that f may be display truth. Selah.

5 That thy delivered; sa hand, and hea

6 God hat holiness, I wi divide Sechem the valley of S

7 Gilead is

asseh is mine, Ephraim also is the strength of mine head; Judah is my law-giver.

8 Moab is my washpot, over Edom will I cast out my shoe: Philistia, triumph thou because of me.

9 Who will bring me into the strong city? who will lead me into Edom?

10 Wilt not thou, O God, which had cast us off? and thou, O God, which didst not go out with our armies?

11 Give us help from trouble: for vain is the help of man.

12 Through God we shall do valiantly: for he it is that shall tread down our enemies.

PSALM LXI.

Hear my cry, O God, attend unto my prayer.

2 From the end of the earth will I cry unto thee, when my heart is overwhelmed: lead me to the rock that is higher than I.

3 For thou hast been a shelter for me, and a strong tower from the enemy.

4 I will abide in thy tabernacle for ever: I will trust in the covert of thy wings. Selah.

5 For thou, O God, hast heard my vows: thou hast given me the heritage of those that fear thy name.

6 Thou wilt prolong the king's life: and his years as many generations.

7 He shall abide before God for ever: O prepare mercy and truth which may preserve him.

8 So will I sing praise unto thy name for ever, that I may daily perform my vows.

PSALM LXII.

Truly my soul waiteth upon God: from him cometh my salvation.

2 He only is my rock and my salvation: he is my defence; I shall not be greatly moved.

3 How long will ye imagine mischief against a man? ye shall be slain all of you: as a bowing wall shall ye be, and as a tottering fence.

4 They only consult to cast him down from his excellency, they delight in lies: they bless with their mouth, but they curse inwardly. Selah.

5 My soul, wait thou only upon God: for my expectation is from him.

6 He only is my rock and my salvation; he is my defence, I shall not be moved.

7 In God is my salvation and my glory: the rock of my strength, and my refuge is in God.

8 Trust in him at all times; ye people, pour out your heart before him: God is a refuge for us. Selah.

9 Surely men of low degree are vanity, and men of high degree are a lie: to be laid in the balance, they are altogether lighter than vanity.

10 Trust not in oppression,

and become not vain in robbery: if riches increase, set not your heart upon them.

11 God hath spoken once; twice have I heard this, that power belongeth unto God.

12 Also unto thee, O Lord, belongeth mercy: for thou renderest to every man according to his work.

PSALM LXIII.

O God, thou art my God, early will I seek thee: my soul thirsteth for thee, my flesh longeth for thee in a dry and thirsty land where no water is:

2 To see thy power and thy glory, so as I have seen thee in the sanctuary.

3 Because thy loving kindness is better than life: my lips shall praise thee.

4 Thus will I bless thee, while I live: I will lift up my hands in thy name.

5 My soul shall be satisfied as with marrow and fatness; and my mouth shall praise thee with joyful lips:

6 When I remember thee upon my bed, and meditate on thee in the night-watches.

7 Because thou hast been my help; therefore in the shadow of thy wings will I rejoice.

8 My soul followeth hard after thee: thy right hand upholdeth me.

9 But those that seek my soul to destroy it, shall go into the lower parts of the earth.

10 They shall fall by the sword, they shall be a portion for foxes.

11 But the king shall rejoice in God, every one that sweareth by him shall glory: but the mouth of them that speak lies shall be stopped.

PSALM LXIV.

HEar my voice, O God, in my prayer; preserve my life from fear of the enemy.

2 Hide me from the secret councel of the wicked; from the insurrection of the workers of iniquity:

3 Who whet their tongue like a sword, and bend their bows to shoot their arrows, even bitter words:

4 That they may shoot in secret at the perfect: suddenly do they shoot at him, and fear not.

5 They encourage themselves in an evil matter: they commune of laying snares privily, they say, Who shall see them?

6 They search out iniquities, they accomplish a diligent search: both the inward thought of every one of them, and the heart is deep.

7 But God shall shoot at them with an arrow, suddenly shall they be wounded.

8 So they shall make their own tongue to fall upon themselves: all that see them shall flee away.

9 And all men shall fear, and shall declare the work of God; for they shall wisely consider of his doing.

10 The righteous shall be glad in the Lord, and shall trust in him; and all the upright in heart shall glory.

PSALM LXV.

PRaise waiteth for thee, O God, in Sion: and unto thee shall the vow be performed.

2 O thou that hearest prayer, unto thee shall all flesh come.

3 Iniquities prevail against me: as for our transgressions thou shalt purge them away.

4 Blessed is the man whom thou choosest and causest to approach unto thee, that he may dwell in thy courts: we shall be satisfied with the goodness of thy house, even of thy holy temple.

5 By terrible things in righteousness, wilt thou answer us, O God of our salvation: who art the confidence of all the ends of the earth, and of them that are afar off upon the sea.

6 Which by his strength setteth fast the mountains; being girded with power.

7 Which stilleth the noise of the seas, the noise of their waves, and the tumult of the people.

8 They also that dwell in the uttermost parts are afraid at thy tokens: thou makest the outgoings of the morning and evening to rejoice.

9 Thou visitest the earth and waterest it: thou greatly enrichest it with the river of God which is full of water: thou preparest them corn, when thou hast so provided for it.

10 Thou waterest the ridges thereof abundantly: thou settlest the furrows thereof; thou makest it soft with showers, thou blessest the springing thereof.

11 Thou crownest the year with thy goodness, and thy paths drop fatness.

12 They drop upon the pastures of the wilderness: and the little hills rejoice on every side.

13 The pastures are clothed with flocks; the vallies also are covered over with corn; they shout for joy, they also sing.

PSALM LXVI.

MAke a joyful noise unto God, all ye lands.

2 Sing forth the honour of his name; make his praise glorious.

3 Say unto God, How terrible art thou in thy works! through the greatness of thy power shall thine enemies submit themselves unto thee:

4 All the earth shall worship thee, and shall sing unto thee: they shall sing to thy name. Selah.

5 Come and see the works of God: he is terrible in his doing toward the children of men.

6 He turned the sea into dry land: they went through the flood on foot, there did we re-

joice in him.

7 He ruleth by his power for ever, his eyes behold the nations; let not the rebellious exalt themselves. Selah.

3 O bless our God, ye people, and make the voice of his praise to be heard.

9 Which holdeth our soul in life, and suffereth not our feet to be moved.

10 For thou, O God, hast proved us: thou hast tried us, as silver is tried.

11 Thou broughtest us into the net, thou laidst affliction upon our loins.

12 Thou hast caused men to ride over our heads; we went through fire and through water: but thou broughtest us out into a wealthy place.

13 I will go into thy house with burnt offerings: I will pay thee my vows,

14 Which my lips have uttered, and my mouth hath spoken when I was in trouble.

15 I will offer unto thee burnt sacrifices of fatlings, with the incense of rams: I will offer bullocks with goats. Selah.

16 Come and hear, all ye that fear God, and I will declare what he hath done for my soul.

17 I cried unto him with my mouth, and he was extolled with my tongue.

18 If I regard iniquity in my heart: the Lord will not hear me.

19 But ve heard me: he the voice of my

20 Blessed hath not turne er, nor his me

PSAL
GOD be and ble his face to shin

2 That th known upon e health among

3 Let the p O God; let praise thee.

4 O let the and sing for jo judge the pec and govern th earth. Selah.

5 Let the thee, O God ple praise thee

6 Then sha her increase; our own God,

7 God sha all the ends fear him.

PSAL
LET Go enemie let them als flee before hi

2 As smok so drive then melteth befor the wicked p sence of God.

3 But let

glad: let them rejoice before God, yea, let them exceedingly rejoice.

4 Sing unto God, sing praises to his Name: extol him that rideth upon the heavens by his name JAH, and rejoice before him.

5 A father of the fatherless, and a judge of the widows, is God in his holy habitation.

6 God setteth the solitary in families: he bringeth out those which are bound with chains, but the rebellious dwell in a dry land.

7 O God, when thou wentest forth before thy people; when thou didst march through the wilderness. Selah.

8 The earth shook, the heavens also dropped at the presence of God: even Sinai itself was moved at the presence of God, the God of Israel.

9 Thou, O God, didst send a plentiful rain, whereby thou didst confirm thine inheritance, when it was weary.

10 Thy congregation hath dwelt therein: thou, O God, hast prepared of thy goodness for the poor.

11 The Lord gave the word: great was the company of those that published it.

12 Kings of armies did flee apace: and she that tarried at home, divided the spoil.

13 Though ye have lien among the pots, yet shall ye be as the wings of a dove covered with silver, and her feathers with yellow gold.

14 When the Almighty scattered kings in it, it was white as snow in Salmon.

15 The hill of God is as the hill of Bashan, an high hill as the hill of Bashan.

16 Why leap ye, ye high hills? this is the hill which God desireth to dwell in, yea, the Lord will dwell in it for ever.

17 The chariots of God are twenty thousand, even thousands of angels: the Lord is among them as in Sinai, in the holy place.

18 Thou hast ascended on high, thou hast led captivity captive: thou hast received gifts of men; yea, for the rebellious also, that the Lord God might dwell among them.

19 Blessed be the Lord, who daily loadeth us with benefits, even the God of our salvation. Selah.

20 He that is our God, is the God of salvation; and unto God the Lord belong the issues from death.

21 But God shall wound the head of his enemies: and the hairy scalp of such a one as goeth on still in his trespasses.

22 The Lord said, I will bring again from Bashan, I will bring my people again from the depths of the sea:

D

23 That thy foot may be dipped in the blood of thine enemies, and the tongue of thy dogs in the same.

24 They have seen thy goings, O God, even the goings of my God, my King, in the sanctuary.

25 The singers went before, the players on instruments followed after; amongst them were the damsels playing with timbrels.

26 Bless ye God in the congregations, even the Lord, from the fountain of Israel.

27 There is little Benjamin with their ruler, the princes of Judah and their counsel, the princes of Zebulun, and the princes of Naphtali.

28 Thy God hath commanded thy strength: strengthen, O God, that which thou hast wrought for us.

29 Because of thy temple at Jerusalem, shall kings bring presents unto thee.

30 Rebuke the company of spearmen, the multitude of the bulls, with the calves of the people, till every one submit himself with pieces of silver: scatter thou the people that delight in war.

31 Princes shall come out of Egypt, Ethiopia shall soon stretch out her hands unto God.

32 Sing unto God, ye kingdoms of the earth: O sing praises unto the Lord. Selah:

33 To him that rideth upon the heavens of heavens, which were of old; lo, he doth send out his voice, and that a mighty voice.

34 Ascribe ye strength unto God: his excellency is over Israel, and his strength is in the clouds.

35 O God, thou art terrible out of thy holy places, the God of Israel is he that giveth strength and power unto his people: blessed be God.

PSALM LXIX.

SAve me, O God, for the waters are come in unto my soul.

2 I sink in deep mire, where there is no standing: I am come into deep waters, where the floods overflow me.

3 I am weary of my crying, my throat is dried: mine eyes fail while I wait for my God.

4 They that hate me without a cause, are more than the hairs of mine head: they that would destroy me being mine enemies wrongfully, are mighty: then I restored that which I took not away.

5 O God, thou knowest my foolishness; and my sins are not hid from thee.

6 Let not them that wait on thee, O Lord God of hosts, be ashamed for my sake: let not those that seek thee, be confounded for my sake, O God of Israel.

7 Because for thy sake I

The NEW-ENGLAND PSALTER.

have borne reproach: shame hath covered my face.

8 I am become a stranger unto my brethren, and an alien unto my mother's children.

9 For the zeal of thine house hath eaten me up: and the reproaches of them that reproached thee, are fallen upon me.

10 When I wept and chastened my soul with fasting, that was to my reproach.

11 I made sackcloth also my garment: and I became a proverb to them.

12 They that sit in the gate speak against me; and I was the song of the drunkards.

13 But as for me, my prayer is unto thee, O Lord, in an acceptable time: O God, in the multitude of thy mercy hear me, in the truth of thy salvation.

14 Deliver me out of the mire, and let me not sink: let me be delivered from them that hate me, and out of the deep waters.

15 Let not the water-flood overflow me, neither let the deep swallow me up, and let not the pit shut her mouth upon me.

16 Hear me, O Lord, for thy loving-kindness is good: turn unto me according to the multitude of thy tender mercies.

17 And hide not thy face from thy servant, for I am in trouble: hear me speedily.

18 Draw nigh unto my soul, and redeem it: deliver me because of mine enemies.

19 Thou hast known my reproach, and my shame, and my dishonour: mine adversaries are all before thee.

20 Reproach hath broken my heart, and I am full of heaviness: and I looked for some to take pity, but there was none: and for comforters, but I found none.

21 They gave me also gall for my meat, and in my thirst they gave me vinegar to drink.

22 Let their table become a snare before them: and that which should have been for their welfare, let it become a trap.

23 Let their eyes be darkened that they see not, and make their loins continually to shake.

24 Pour out thine indignation upon them, and let thy wrathful anger take hold of them.

25 Let their habitation be desolate, and let none dwell in their tents.

26 For they persecute him whom thou hast smitten, and they talk to the grief of those whom thou hast wounded.

27 Add iniquity to their iniquity: and let them not come into thy righteousness.

28 Let them be blotted out of the book of the living, and not be written with the righteous.

29 But I am poor and sorrowful: let thy salvation, O

God, set me up on high.

30 I will praise the name of God with a song, and will magnify him with thanksgiving.

31 This also shall please the Lord better than ox or bullock that hath horns and hoofs.

32 The humble shall see this and be glad: and your heart shall live that seek God.

33 For the Lord heareth the poor, and despiseth not his prisoners.

34 Let the heaven and earth praise him, the seas, and every thing that moveth therein.

35 For God will save Sion, and will build the cities of Judah: that they may dwell there, and have it in possession.

36 The seed also of his servants shall inherit it: and they that love his name shall dwell therein.

PSALM LXX.

MAKE haste, O God to deliver me; make haste to help me, O Lord.

2 Let them be ashamed and confounded that seek after my soul: let them be turned backward, and put to confusion, that desire my hurt.

3 Let them be turned back for a reward of their shame that say Aha, aha.

4 Let all those that seek thee rejoice and be glad in thee, and let such as love thy salvation say continually, Let God be magnified.

5 But I am make haste unto thou art my deliverer, O Lord
rying. PSA

IN thee, O my trust, put to confusion

2 Deliver teousness, and cape: incline me and save me

3 Be thou tion whereunto ally resort: commandmen thou art my trefs.

4 Deliver out of the hand out of the hand teous and cru

5 For thou Lord God: from my you

6 By thee en up from art he that to mother's bo shall be conti

7 I am as many; but t refuge.

8 Let my h thy pr h ur all th Cast me of old ag when my st

10 For m against me:

wait for my soul take counsel together

11 Saying God hath forsaken him : persecute and take him, for there is none to deliver him.

12 O God, be not far from me : O my God, make haste for my help.

13 Let them be confounded and consumed, that are adversaries to my soul : let them be covered with reproach and dishonour, that seek my hurt.

14 But I will hope continually, and will yet praise thee more and more.

15 My mouth shall shew forth thy righteousness, and thy salvation all the day : for I know not the numbers thereof.

16 I will go in the strength of the Lord God : I will make mention of thy righteousness, even of thine only.

17 O God thou hast taught me from my youth : and hitherto have I declared thy wondrous works.

18 Now also when I am old and grey-headed, O God forsake me not : until I have shewed thy strength unto this generation, and thy power to every one that is to come.

19 Thy righteousness also, O God, is very high, who hast done great things : O God, who is like unto thee?

20 Thou which hast shewed me great and sore troubles, shalt quicken me again, and shalt bring me up again from the depths of the earth.

21 Thou shalt increase my greatness, and comfort me on every side.

22 I will also praise thee with the psaltery, even thy truth, O my God : Unto thee will I sing with the harp, O thou holy One of Israel.

23 My lips shall greatly rejoice when I sing unto thee: and my soul which thou hast redeemed.

24 My tongue also shall talk of thy righteousness all the day long : for they are confounded, for they are brought unto shame, that seek my hurt.

PSALM LXXII.

Give the king thy judgments, O God, and thy righteousness unto the king's son.

2 He shall judge thy people with righteousness, and thy poor with judgment.

3 The mountains shall bring peace to the people, and the little hills by righteousness.

4 He shall judge the poor of the people, he shall save the children of the needy, and shall break in pieces the oppressor.

5 They shall fear thee as long as the sun and moon endure, throughout all generations.

6 He shall come down like rain upon the mown grass : as showers that water the earth.

7 In his days shall the righteous flourish : and abundance

of peace so long as the moon endureth.

8 He shall have dominion also from sea to sea, and from the river unto the ends of the earth.

9 They that dwell in the wilderness shall bow before him: and his enemies shall lick the dust.

10 The kings of Tarshish and of the isles shall bring presents: the kings of Sheba and Seba shall offer gifts.

11 Yea, all kings shall fall down before him: all nations shall serve him.

12 For he shall deliver the needy when he crieth: the poor also, and him that hath no helper.

13 He shall spare the poor and ——, and shall save the souls of the needy.

14 He shall redeem their soul from deceit and violence: and precious shall their blood be in his sight.

15 And he shall live, and to him shall be given of the gold of Sheba; prayer also shall be made for him continually, and daily shall he be praised.

16 There shall be an handful of corn in the earth upon the top of the mountains: the

men shall be bl
nations shall ca
18 Blessed b
the God of I
doth wondrous
19 And bl
rious name fo
the whole eart
his glory; An
20 The pr
the son of Jesse

PSALM
TRuly Go
real, ev
of a clean heart
2 But as fo
were almost
had well nigh
3 For I wa
foolish, when
perity of the w
4 For there
their death: b
is firm.
5 They are
other men:
plagued like ot
6 Therefor
seth them ab
violence cove
garment.
7 Their ey
fatness: they
heart could wi

turn hither: and waters of a full cup are wrung out to them.

11 And they say, How doth God know? and is there knowledge in the most High?

12 Behold, these are the ungodly, who prosper in the world, they increase in riches.

13 Verily, I have cleansed my heart in vain, and washed my hands in innocency.

14 For all the day long have I been plagued, and chastened every morning.

15 If I say, I will speak thus: behold I should offend against the generation of thy children.

16 When I thought to know this, it was too painful for me.

17 Until I went into the sanctuary of God; then understood I their end.

18 Surely thou didst set them in slippery places: thou castedst them down into destruction.

19 How are they brought into desolation, as in a moment! they are utterly consumed with terrors.

20 As a dream when one awaketh; so, O Lord, when thou awakest thou shalt despise their image.

21 Thus my heart was grieved, and I was pricked in my reins.

24 Thou shalt guide me with thy counsel, and afterwards receive me to glory.

25 Whom have I in heaven but thee? and there is none upon earth that I desire besides thee.

26 My flesh and my heart faileth: but God is the strength of my heart, and my portion for ever.

27 For lo, they that are far from thee, shall perish: thou hast destroyed all them that go a whoring from thee.

28 But it is good for me to draw near to God; I have put my trust in the Lord God, that I may declare all thy works.

PSALM LXXIV.

O God, why hast thou cast us off for ever? why doth thine anger smoke against the sheep of thy pasture?

2 Remember thy congregation which thou hast purchased of old: the rod of thine inheritance which thou hast redeemed, this mount Zion wherein thou hast dwelt.

3 Lift up thy feet unto the perpetual desolations: even all that the enemy hath done wickedly in the sanctuary.

4 Thine enemies roar in the midst of thy congregations: they

with axes and hammers.

7 They have cast fire into thy sanctuary, they have defiled by casting down the dwelling-place of thy name to the ground.

8 They said in their hearts, Let us destroy them together: they have burnt up all the synagogues of God in the land.

9 We see not our signs, there is no more any prophet, neither is there among us any that knoweth how long.

10 O God, how long shall the adversary reproach? shall the enemy blaspheme thy name for ever?

11 Why withdrawest thou thy hand, even thy right hand? pluck it out of thy bosom.

12 For God is my King of old, working salvation in the midst of the earth.

13 Thou didst divide the sea: by thy strength thou breakest the heads of the dragons in the waters.

14 Thou breakest the heads of leviathan in pieces, & gavest him to be meat to the people inhabiting the wilderness.

15 Thou didst cleave the fountain and the flood: thou driedst up mighty rivers.

16 The day is thine, the enemy hath reproached, O Lord, and that the foolish people have blasphemed thy name.

19 O deliver not the soul of thy turtle-dove unto the multitude of the wicked, forget not the congregation of thy poor for ever.

20 Have respect unto the covenant: for the dark places of the earth are full of the habitations of cruelty.

21 O let not the oppressed return ashamed: let the poor and needy praise thy name.

22 Arise, O God, plead thine own cause: remember how the foolish man reproacheth thee daily.

23 Forget not the voice of thine enemies: the tumult of those that rise up against thee, increaseth continually.

PSALM LXXV.

UNto thee, O God, do we give thanks, unto thee do we give thanks: for that thy name is near, thy wondrous works declare.

2 When I shall receive the congregation, I will judge uprightly.

3 The earth and all the inhabitants thereof are dissolved: I bear up the pillars of it. Selah.

neither from the east, nor from the west, nor from the south.

7 But God is the judge : he putteth down one and setteth up another.

8 For in the hand of the Lord there is a cup, and the wine is red : it is full of mixture, and he poureth out of the same : but the dregs thereof all the wicked of the earth shall wring them out and drink them.

9 But I will declare for ever ; I will sing praises to the God of Jacob.

10 All the horns of the wicked also will I cut off ; but the horns of the righteous shall be exalted.

PSALM LXXVI.

IN Judah is God known : his name is great in Israel.

2 In Salem also is his tabernacle, and his dwelling-place in Zion.

3 There brake he the arrows of the bow, the shield, and the sword, and the battle. Selah.

4 Thou art more glorious and excellent than the mountains of prey.

5 The stout-hearted are spoiled, they have slept their sleep : and none of the men of might have found their hands.

6 At thy rebuke, O God of Jacob, both the chariot and horse are cast into a dead sleep.

7 Thou, even thou art to be feared, and who may stand in thy sight when once thou art angry ?

8 Thou didst cause judgment to be heard from heaven ; the earth feared and was still,

9 When God arose to judgment to save all the meek of the earth. Selah.

10 Surely the wrath of man shall praise thee : the remainder of wrath shalt thou restrain.

11 Vow, and pay unto the Lord your God ; let all that be around about him bring presents unto him that ought to be feared.

12 He shall cut off the spirit of princes : he is terrible to the kings of the earth.

PSALM LXXVII.

I Cried unto God with my voice : even unto God with my voice, and he gave ear unto me.

2 In the day of my trouble I sought the Lord : my sore ran in the night, and ceased not : my soul refused to be comforted

3 I remembered God, and was troubled : I complained, and my spirit was overwhelmed. Selah.

4 Thou holdest mine eyes waking : I am so troubled that I cannot speak.

5 I have considered the days of old, the years of ancient times.

6 I call to remembrance my song in the night : I commune with mine own heart, and my spirit made diligent search.

7 Will the Lord cast off for ever ? and will he be favour-

able no more?

8 Is his mercy clean gone for ever? doth his promise fail for evermore?

9 Hath God forgotten to be gracious? hath he in anger shut up his tender mercies? Selah.

10 And I said, This is my infirmity: but I will remember the years of the right hand of the most High.

11 I will remember the works of the Lord: surely I will remember thy wonders of old.

12 I will meditate also of all thy work, & talk of thy doings.

13 Thy way, O God, is in the sanctuary: who is so great a God as our God?

14 Thou art the God that doest wonders; thou hast declared thy strength among the people.

15 Thou hast with thine arm redeemed thy people, the sons of Jacob and Joseph. Selah.

16 The waters saw thee, O God, the waters saw thee: they were afraid: the depths also were troubled.

17 The clouds poured out water, the skies sent out a sound: thine arrows also went abroad.

18 The voice of thy thunder was in the heaven: the lightnings lightned the world, the earth trembled and shook.

19 Thy way is in the sea and thy path in the great waters and thy foot-steps are not known.

20 Thou leddest thy people like a flock, by the hand of Moses and Aaron.

'PSALM LXXVIII.

Give ear, O my people, to my law: incline your ears, to the words of my mouth.

2 I will open my mouth in a parable: I will utter dark sayings of old:

3 Which we have heard and known, and our fathers have told us.

4 We will not hide them from their children, shewing to the generation to come, the praises of the Lord; and his strength and his wonderful works that he hath done.

5 For he established a testimony in Jacob, and appointed a law in Israel, which he commanded our fathers, that they should make them known to their children.

6 That the generation to come might know them, even the children which should be born: who should arise and declare them to their children:

7 That they might set their hope in God, and not forget the works of God; but keep his commandments:

8 And might not be as their fathers, a stubborn and rebellious generation; a generation that set not their heart aright, and whose spirit was not stedfast with God.

9 The children of Ephraim being armed and carrying bows,

The New-England Psalter.

turned back in the day of battle.

10 They kept not the covenant of God, and refused to walk in his law:

11 And forgat his works and his wonders that he had shewed them.

12 Marvellous things did he in the sight of their fathers, in the land of Egypt, in the field of Zoan.

13 He divided the sea, and caused them to pass through, and he made the waters to stand as an heap.

14 In the day time also he led them with a cloud, and all the night with a light of fire.

15 He clave the rocks in the wilderness, and gave them drink as out of the great depths.

16 He brought streams also out of the rock, and caused waters to run down like rivers.

17 And they sinned yet more against him, by provoking the most High in the wilderness.

18 And they tempted God in their heart, by asking meat for their lust.

19 Yea, they spake against God: they said, Can God furnish a table in the wilderness?

20 Behold, he smote the rock, that the waters gushed

anger also came up against Israel:

22 Because they believed not in God, and trusted not in his salvation:

23 Though he had commanded the clouds from above, and opened the doors of heaven.

24 And had rained down manna upon them to eat, and had given them of the corn of heaven.

25 Man did eat angels food: he sent them meat to the full.

26 He caused an east wind to blow in the heaven: and by his power he brought in the south wind.

27 He rained flesh also upon them as dust, and feathered fowls like as the sand of the sea.

28 And he let it fall in the midst of their camp, round about their habitations.

29 So they did eat, and were well filled, for he gave them their own desire;

30 They were not estranged from their lusts: but while their meat was yet in their mouths.

31 The wrath of God came upon them and slew the fattest of them, and smote down the chosen men of Israel.

32 For all this they sinned still, and believed not for his

returned, and enquired early after God.

35 And they remembered that God was their rock, and the high God their redeemer.

36 Nevertheless they did flatter him with their mouth, and they lied unto him with their tongues.

37 For their heart was not right with him, neither were they stedfast in his covenant.

38 But he being full of compassion, forgave their iniquity, and destroyed them not; yea, many a time turned he his anger away, and did not stir up all his wrath.

39 For he remembered that they were but flesh; a wind that passeth away, and cometh not again.

40 How oft did they provoke him in the wilderness, and grieve him in the desart?

41 Yea, they turned back and tempted God, and limited the holy One of Israel.

42 They remembered not his hand, nor the day when he delivered them from the enemy.

43 How he had wrought his signs in Egypt, and his wonders in the field of Zoan.

44 And had turned their rivers into blood, & their floods, that they could not drink.

45 He sent divers sorts of flies among them, which devoured them; and frogs, which destroyed them.

46 He gave also their increase unto the caterpillar, and their labour unto the locust.

47 He destroyed their vines with hail, and their sycamore trees with frost.

48 He gave up their cattle also to the hail, and their flocks to hot thunder-bolts.

49 He cast upon them the fierceness of his anger, wrath and indignation, and trouble, by sending evil angels among them.

50 He made a way to his anger, he spared not their soul from death: but gave their life over to the pestilence.

51 And smote all the first-born in Egypt: the chief of their strength in the tabernacles of Ham:

52 But made his own people to go forth like sheep, and guided them in the wilderness like a flock.

53 And he led them on safely, so that they feared not: but the sea overwhelmed their enemies.

54 And he brought them to the border of his sanctuary, even to this mountain, which his right hand had purchased.

55 He cast out the heathen also before them, and divided them an inheritance by line, and made the tribes of Israel to dwell in their tents.

56 Yet they tempted and provoked the most high God,

and kept not his testimonies:

57 But turned back and dealt unfaithfully like their fathers: they were turned aside like a deceitful bow.

58 For they provoked him to anger with her high places, and moved him to jealousy with their graven images.

59 When God heard this, he was wroth, and greatly abhorred Israel:

60 So that he forsook the tabernacle of Shiloh, the tent which he placed among men:

61 And delivered his strength into captivity, and his glory into the enemies hand.

62 He gave his people over also unto the sword: and was wroth with his inheritance.

63 The fire consumed their young men; and their maidens were not given to marriage.

64 Their priests fell by the sword: and their widows made no lamentation.

65 Then the Lord awaked as one out of sleep, and like a mighty man that shouteth by reason of wine.

66 And he smote his enemies in the hinder parts: he put them to a perpetual reproach.

67 Moreover, he refused the tabernacle of Joseph, and chose not the tribe of Ephraim.

68 But chose the tribe of Judah, the mount Zion, which he loved.

69 And he built his sanctuary like high palaces, like the earth which he hath established for ever.

70 He chose David also his servant and took him from the sheep-folds:

71 From following the ewes great with young, he brought him to feed Jacob his people, and Israel his inheritance.

72 So he fed them according to the integrity of his heart: and guided them by the skilfulness of his hands.

PSALM LXXIX.

O God, the heathen are come into thine inheritance, thy holy temple have they defiled: they have laid Jerusalem in heaps.

2 The dead bodies of thy servants have they given to be meat unto the fowls of the heaven, the flesh of thy saints unto the beasts of the earth.

3 Their blood have they shed like water round about Jerusalem: and there was none to bury them.

4 We are become a reproach to our neighbours: a scorn and derision to them that are round about us.

5 How long, Lord? wilt thou be angry for ever? shall thy jealousy burn like fire?

6 Pour out thy wrath upon the heathen that have not known thee, and upon the kingdoms that have not called upon thy name.

7 For they have devoured Jacob, and laid waste his dwelling-place.

8 O remember not against us former iniquites: let thy tender mercies speedily prevent us: for we are brought very low.

9 Help us, O God of our salvation, for the glory of thy name: and deliver us, and purge away our sins for thy names sake.

10 Wherefore should the heathen say, Where is their God? let him be known among the heathen in our sight by the revenging of the blood of thy servants which is shed.

11 Let the sighing of the prisoner come before thee, according to the greatness of thy power: preserve thou those that are appointed to die.

12 And render unto our neighbours seven-fold into their bosom, their reproach wherewith they have reproached thee O Lord.

13 So we thy people and sheep of thy pasture, will give thee thanks for ever: we will shew forth thy praise to all generations.

PSALM LXXX.

Give ear, O Shepherd of Israel, thou that leadest Joseph like a flock, thou that dwellest between the cherubims, shine forth.

2 Before Ephraim, and Benjamin, and Manasseh, stir up thy strength, and come and save us.

3 Turn us again, O God and cause thy face to shine, and we shall be saved.

4 O Lord God of hosts, how long wilt thou be angry against the prayer of thy people?

5 Thou feedest them with the bread of tears: and givest them tears to drink in great measure

6 Thou makest us a strife unto our neighbours: and our enemies laugh among themselves

7 Turn us again, O God of hosts, and cause thy face to shine, and we shall be saved.

8 Thou hast brought a vine out of Egypt: thou hast cast out the heathen, and planted it

9 Thou preparedst room before it, and didst cause it to take deep root, and it filled the land

10 The hills were covered with the shadow of it, and the boughs thereof were like the goodly cedars.

11 She sent out her boughs unto the sea, and her branches unto the river.

12 Why hast thou then broken down her hedges, so that all they which pass by the way do pluck her?

13 The boar out of the wood doth waste it, and the wild beast of the field doth devour it.

14 Return, we beseech thee O God of hosts: look down from heaven, and behold, and visit this vine;

15 And the vineyard which thy right hand hath planted

and the branch that thou madeſt ſtrong for thyſelf.

16 It is burnt with fire, it is cut down: they periſh at the rebuke of thy countenance.

17 Let thy hand be upon the man of thy right hand, upon the ſon of man whom thou madeſt ſtrong for thyſelf.

18 So will not we go back from thee: quicken us, and we will call upon thy name.

19 Turn us again, O Lord God of hoſts, cauſe thy face to ſhine, and we ſhall be ſaved.

PSALM LXXXI.

Sing aloud unto God our ſtrength: make a joyful noiſe unto the God of Jacob.

2 Take a pſalm, and bring hither the timbrel, the pleaſant harp with the pſaltery.

3 Blow up the trumpet in the new moon, in the time appointed, on our ſolemn feaſt day.

4 For this was a ſtatute for Iſrael, and a law of the God of Jacob.

5 This he ordained in Joſeph for a teſtimony, when he went out through the land of Egypt: where I heard a language that I underſtood not.

6 I removed his ſhoulder from the burden: his hands were delivered from the pots.

7 Thou calledſt in trouble, and I delivered thee; I anſwered thee in the ſecret place of thunder: I proved thee at the waters of Meribah. Selah.

8 Hear, O my people, and I will teſtify unto thee: O Iſrael, if thou wilt hearken unto me;

9 There ſhall no ſtrange god be in thee: neither ſhall thou worſhip any ſtrange god.

10 I am the Lord thy God which brought thee out of the land of Egypt: open thy mouth wide, and I will fill it.

11 But my people would not hearken to my voice: and Iſrael would none of me.

12 So I gave them up unto their own hearts luſt: and they walked in their own counſels.

13 O that my people had hearkened unto me, and Iſrael had walked in my ways!

14 I ſhould ſoon have ſubdued their enemies, and turned my hand againſt their adverſaries.

15 The haters of the Lord ſhould have ſubmitted themſelves unto him: but their time ſhould have endured for ever.

16 He ſhould have fed them alſo with the fineſt of the wheat: and with honey out of the rock ſhould I have ſatisfied thee.

PSALM LXXXII.

GOD ſtandeth in the congregation of the mighty: he judgeth among the gods.

2 How long will ye judge unjuſtly, and accept the perſons of the wicked? Selah.

3 Defend the poor and fatherleſs: do juſtice to the afflicted and needy.

4 Deliver the poor and needy: rid them out of the hand

of the wicked.

5 They know not, neither will they understand; they walk on in darknefs: all the foundations of the earth are out of courfe.

6 I have faid, Ye are Gods: and all of you are children of the moft High.

7 But ye fhall die like men, and fall like one of the princes.

8 Arife, O God, judge the earth: for thou fhalt inherit all nations.

PSALM LXXXIII.

KEep not thou filence, O God: hold not thy peace, and be not ftill, O God.

2 For, lo, thine enemies make a tumult: and they that hate thee lift up the head.

3 They have taken crafty counfel againft thy people, and confulted againft thy hidden ones.

4 They have faid, Come, and let us cut them off from being a nation: that the name of Ifrael may be no more in remembrance.

5 For they have confulted together with one confent: they are confederate againft thee.

6 The tabernacles of Edom, and the Ifhmaelites: of Moab and the Hagarenes.

7 Gebal, and Ammon, and Amalech, the Philiftines with the inhabitants of Tyre.

8 Affur alfo is joined with them: they have holpen the children of Lot. Selah.

9 Do unto
Midianites: a
Jabin, at the

10 Which
dor: they b
the earth.

11 Make
Oreb, and 1
all their pr
and as Zalm

12 Who f
to ourfelves t
in poffeffion.

13 O my
like a wheel
before the w

14 As the
wood, and a
the mountai

15 So pe
thy tempeft,
afraid with t

16 Fill
fhame: tha
thy name, C

17 Let them
troubled for
be put to fha

18 That
that thou wl
JEHOVAH
over all the

PSAL

HOW a
ernacl

2 My foul
fainteth for
Lord: my
crieth out fo

3 Yea,
found an ho

low a nest for herself, where she may lay her young, even thine altars, O Lord of hosts, my king, and my God.

4. Blessed are they that dwell in thy house: they will be still praising thee. Selah.

5 Blessed is the man whose strength is in thee: in whose heart are the ways of them.

6 Who passing through the valley of Baca, make it a well: the rain also filleth the pools.

7 They go from strength to strength, every one of them in Zion appeareth before God.

8 O Lord God of hosts, hear my prayer: give ear, O God of Jacob. Selah.

9 Behold, O God our shield, and look upon the face of thine anointed.

10 For a day in thy courts is better than a thousand: I had rather be a door-keeper in the house of my God, than to dwell in the tents of wickedness.

11 For the Lord God is a sun and shield: the Lord will give grace and glory: no good thing will he withhold from them that walk uprightly.

12 O Lord of hosts, blessed is the man that trusteth in thee.

PSALM LXXXV.

Lord, thou hast been favourable unto thy land: thou hast brought back the captivity of Jacob.

2 Thou hast forgiven the iniquity of thy people, thou hast covered all their sin. Selah.

3 Thou hast taken away all thy wrath: thou hast turned thyself from the fierceness of thine anger.

4 Turn us, O God of our salvation, and cause thine anger towards us to cease.

5 Wilt thou be angry with us for ever? wilt thou draw out thine anger to all generations?

6 Wilt thou not revive us again: that thy people may rejoice in thee?

7 Shew us thy mercy, O Lord, and grant us thy salvation.

8 I will hear what God the Lord will speak: for he will speak peace unto his people, and to his saints: but let them not turn again to folly.

9 Surely his salvation is nigh them that fear him: that glory may dwell in our land.

10 Mercy and truth are met together: righteousness and peace have kissed each other.

11 Truth shall spring out of the earth: and righteousness shall look down from heaven.

12 Yea, the Lord shall give that which is good: and our land shall yield her increase.

13 Righteousness shall go before him: and shall set us in the way of his steps.

PSALM LXXXVI.

Bow down thine ear, O Lord, hear me: for I am poor and needy.

2 Preserve my soul, for I am holy:

holy: O thou my God, save thy servant that trusteth in thee.

3 Be merciful unto me, O Lord: for I cry unto thee daily.

4 Rejoice the soul of thy servant: for unto thee, O Lord, do I lift up my soul.

5 For thou, Lord, art good, and ready to forgive: and plenteous in mercy unto all them that call upon thee.

6 Give ear, O Lord, unto my prayer: and attend to the voice of my supplications.

7 In the day of my trouble I will call upon thee: for thou wilt answer me.

8 Among the gods there is none like unto thee, O Lord, neither are there any works like unto thy works.

9 All nations whom thou hast made shall come and worship before thee, O Lord: and shall glorify thy name.

10 For thou art great, and doest wondrous things: thou art God alone.

11 Teach me thy way, O Lord, I will walk in thy truth: unite my heart to fear thy name.

12 I will praise thee, O Lord my God, with all my heart: and I will glorify thy name for evermore.

13 For great is thy mercy toward me: and thou hast delivered my soul from the lowest hell.

14 O God, the proud are risen against me, and the assemblies of violent men have sought after my soul: and have not set thee before them.

15 But thou, O Lord, art a God full of compassion, and gracious: long-suffering, and plenteous in mercy and truth.

16 O turn unto me and have mercy upon me, give thy strength unto thy servant, and save the son of thine handmaid.

17 Shew me a token for good, that they which hate me may see it, and be ashamed: because thou, Lord, hast holpen me, and comforted me.

PSALM LXXXVII.

HIS foundation is in the holy mountains.

2 The Lord loveth the gates of Zion, more than all the dwellings of Jacob.

3 Glorious things are spoken of thee, O city of God. Selah.

4 I will make mention of Rahab, and Babylon, to them that know me; behold Philistia, and Tyre, with Ethiopia: this man was born there.

5 And of Zion it shall be said, This and that man was born in her: and the Highest himself shall establish her.

6 The Lord shall count when he writeth up the people, that this man was born there. Selah.

7 As well the singers as the players on instruments shall be there: all my springs are in thee.

NEW-ENGLAND PSALTER.

XXXVIII.
of my falva-
ye cried day
hee.
yer come be-
ne thine ear

il is full of
life draweth
ve.
d with them
o the pit : I
hat hath no

the dead,
at lie in the
remembreft
ey are cut off

id me in the
knefs, in the

ieth hard up-
haft afflicted
ives. Selah.
it away mine
from me :
an abomin-
. I am fhut
ome forth.
nourneth by
n : Lord, I
upon thee, I
it my hands

hew wonders
all the dead
e ? Selah.
loving-kind
n the grave ?
in deftruc-

tion?

12 Shall thy worders be known in the dark? and thy righteoufnefs in the hand of forgetfulnefs?

13 But unto thee have I cried, O Lord, and in the morning fhall my prayer prevent thee.

14 Lord, why cafteft thou off my foul? why hideft thou thy face from me?

15 I am afflicted and ready to die, from my youth up: while I fuffer thy terrors I am diftracted.

16 Thy fierce wrath goeth over me, thy terrors have cut me off.

17 They came round about me daily like water, they compaffed me about together.

18 Lover and friend haft thou put far from me, and mine acquaintance into darknefs.

PSALM LXXXIX.

I Will fing of the mercies of the Lord forever: with my mouth will I make known thy faithfulnefs to all generations.

2 For I have faid, Mercy fhall be built up for ever: thy faithfulnefs fhalt thou eftablifh in the very heavens.

3 I have made a covenant with my chofen, I have fworn unto David my fervant.

4 Thy feed will I eftablifh for ever, and build up thy throne to all generations. Selah.

5 And the heavens shall praise thy wonders, O Lord: thy faithfulness also in the congregation of the saints.

6 For who in the heaven can be compared unto the Lord? who among the sons of the mighty can be likened unto the Lord?

7 God is greatly to be feared in the assembly of the saints: and to be had in reverence of all them that are about him.

8 O Lord God of hosts, who is a strong Lord like unto thee? or to thy faithfulness round about thee?

9 Thou rulest the raging of the sea: when the waves thereof arise thou stillest them.

10 Thou hast broken Rahab in pieces, as one that is slain; thou hast scattered thine enemies with thy strong arm.

11 The heavens are thine, the earth also is thine: as for the world and the fulness thereof, thou hast founded them.

12 The north and the south thou hast created them: Tabor and Hermon shall rejoice in thy name.

13 Thou hast a mighty arm: strong is thy hand, and high is thy right hand.

14 Justice and judgment are the habitation of thy throne: mercy and truth shall go before thy face.

15 Blessed is the people that know the joyful sound: they shall walk, O

light of thy cou

16 In thy nam joice all the day teousness shall t

17 For thou their strength: a our horn shall l

18 For the fence: and the rael is our king

19 Then thou on to the holy I have laid hel is mighty: I h chosen out of t

20 I have f servant: with 1 I anointed him

21 With v shall be establis also shall streng

22 The ene act upon him: wickedness aff

23 And I w foes before his them that hat

24 But my my mercy sha and in my nar be exalted.

25 I will se the sea, and h the rivers.

26 He sha Thou art my and the rock o

27 Also I w first-bo n. hi kings of the c

28 My mercy will I keep for him for evermore, and my covenant shall stand fast with him.

29. His seed also will I make to endure for ever, and his throne as the days of heaven.

30 If his children forsake my law, and walk not in my judgments;

31 If they break my statutes, and keep not my commandments;

32 Then will I visit their transgression with the rod, and their iniquity with stripes.

33 Nevertheless, my loving kindness will I not utterly take from him, nor suffer my faithfulness to fail.

34 My covenant will I not break, nor alter the thing that is gone out of my lips.

35 Once have I sworn by my holiness, that I will not lie unto David.

36 His seed shall endure for ever, and his throne as the sun before me.

37 It shall be established for ever as the moon, and as a faithful witness in heaven. Selah.

38 But thou hast cast off and abhorred, thou hast been wrath with thine anointed.

39 Thou hast made void the covenant of thy servant: thou hast profaned his crown, by casting it to the ground.

40 Thou hast broken down all his hedges, thou hast brought his strong holds to ruin.

41 All that pass by the way spoil him: he is a reproach to his neighbours.

42 Thou hast set up the right hand of his adversaries: thou hast made all his enemies to rejoice.

43 Thou hast also turned the edge of his sword, and hast not made him to stand in the battle.

44 Thou hast made his glory to cease, and cast his throne down to the ground.

45 The days of his youth hast thou shortened: thou hast covered him with shame. Selah.

46 How long, Lord, wilt thou hide thyself for ever? shall thy wrath burn like fire?

47 Remember how short my time is; wherefore hast thou made all men in vain?

48 What man is he that liveth, and shall not see death? shall he deliver his soul from the hand of the grave? Selah.

49 Lord, where are thy former loving kindnesses, which thou swearest unto David in thy truth?

50 Remember, Lord, the reproach of thy servants; how I do bear in my bosom the reproach of all the mighty people;

51 Wherewith thine enemies have reproached, O Lord; wherewith they have reproached the footsteps of thine anointed.

52 Blessed be the Lord for evermore. Amen, and Amen.

PSALM XC.

Lord, thou haſt been our dwelling-place in all generations.

2 Before the mountains were brought forth, or ever thou hadſt formed the earth and the world: even from everlaſting to everlaſting, thou art God.

3 Thou turneſt man to deſtruction: and ſayeſt, Return, ye children of men.

4 For a thouſand years in thy ſight are but as yeſterday when it is paſt, and as a watch in the night.

5 Thou carrieſt them away as with a flood, they are as a ſleep: in the morning they are like graſs which groweth up.

6 In the morning it flouriſheth, and groweth up; in the evening it is cut down and withereth.

7 For we are conſumed by thine anger, and by thy wrath are we troubled.

8 Thou haſt ſet our iniquities before thee, our ſecret ſins in the light of thy countenance.

9 For all our days are paſſed away in thy wrath: we ſpend our years as a tale that is told.

10 The days of our years are three-ſcore years and ten: and if, by reaſon of ſtrength, they be four-ſcore years, yet is their ſtrength labour and ſorrow; for it is ſoon cut off, and and we fly away.

11 Who knoweth the power of thine anger
ing to thy fear

12 So teach
our days, that
our hearts unto

13 Return,
long? and le
concerning thy

14 O ſatisfy
thy mercy;
joice and be gl

15 Make us
to the days v
afflicted us,
wherein we h

16 Let thy
to thy ſervants
unto their chil

17 And let
lord our God
eſtabliſh thou
hands upon u
of our hands e

PSA

He that
ſecret
High, ſhall
ſhadow of the

2 I will ſay
my refuge and
God in him w

3 Surely he
from the ſnare
from the noiſe

4 He ſhall
his feathers,
wings ſhalt
truth ſhall be
buckler.

5 Thou ſ
for the terror

PSALM XCII.

1 IT is a good thing to give thanks unto the Lord, and to sing praises unto thy name O most High;

2 To shew forth thy loving-kindness in the morning, and thy faithfulness every night:

3 Upon an instrument of ten strings, and upon the psaltery; upon the harp with a solemn sound.

4 For thou Lord, hast made me glad through thy work: I will triumph in the works of thy hands.

5 O Lord, how great are thy works! and thy thoughts are very deep.

6 A brutish man knoweth not: neither doth a fool understand this.

7 When the wicked spring as the grass, and when all the workers of iniquity do flourish: it is, that they shall be destroyed for ever.

8 But thou, Lord art most high for evermore.

9 For lo, thine enemies, O Lord, for lo, thine enemies shall perish: all the workers of iniquity shall be scattered.

10 But my horn shalt thou exalt like the horn of an unicorn: I shall be anointed with fresh oil.

11 Mine eye also shall see my desire on mine enemies: and mine ears shall hear my desire of the wicked that rise up

against me.

12 The righteous shall flourish like the palm-tree: he shall grow like a cedar in Lebanon.

13 Those that be planted in the house of the Lord, shall flourish in the courts of our God.

14 They shall still bring forth fruit in old age: they shall be fat, and flourishing.

15 To shew that the Lord is upright: he is my rock, and there is no unrighteousness in him.

PSALM XCIII.

THE Lord reigneth, he is cloathed with majesty, the Lord is cloathed with strength, wherewith he hath girded himself: the world also is established, that it cannot be moved.

2 Thy throne is established of old: thou art from everlasting.

3 The floods have lifted up, O Lord, the floods have lifted up their voice: the floods lift up their waves.

4 The Lord on high is mightier than the noise of many waters, yea, than the mighty waves of the sea.

5 Thy testimonies are very sure: holiness becometh thine house, O Lord for ever.

PSALM XCIV.

O Lord God, to whom vengeance belongeth; O God, to whom vengeance belongeth, shew thyself.

2 Lift up thyself, thou judge of the earth: render a reward to the proud.

3 Lord, how long shall the wicked, how long shall the wicked triumph?

4 How long shall they utter and speak hard things? and all the workers of iniquity boast themselves?

5 They break in pieces thy people, O Lord, and afflict thine heritage.

6 They slay the widow and the stranger, and murder the fatherless.

7 Yet they say, The Lord shall not see: neither shall the God of Jacob regard it.

8 Understand, ye brutish among the people: and ye fools, when will ye be wise?

9 He that planted the ear, shall he shall not hear? he that formed the eye, shall he not see?

10 He that chastiseth the heathen, shall not he correct? he that teacheth man knowledge, shall not he know?

11 The Lord knoweth the thoughts of man, that they are vanity.

12 Blessed is the man whom thou chastnest, O Lord, and teachest him out of thy law:

13 That thou mayest give him rest from the days of adversity, until the pit be digged for the wicked.

14 For the Lord will not

cast off his people, neither will he forsake his inheritance.

15 But judgment shall return unto righteousness: and all the upright in heart shall follow it.

16 Who will rise up for me against the evil-doers? or who will stand up for me against the workers of iniquity?

17 Unless the Lord had been my help, my soul had almost dwelt in silence.

18 When I said, My foot slippeth: thy mercy, O Lord, held me up.

19 In the multitude of my thoughts within me, thy comforts delight my soul.

20 Shall the throne of iniquity have fellowship with thee, which frameth mischief by a law?

21 They gather themselves together against the soul of the righteous, and condemn the innocent blood.

22 But the Lord is my defence: and my God is the rock of my refuge.

23 And he shall bring upon them their own iniquity, and shall cut them off in their own wickedness; yea, the Lord our God shall cut them off.

PSLAM XCV.

O Come, let us sing unto the Lord; let us make a joyful noise to the rock of our salvation.

2 Let us come before his presence with thanksgiving, and make a joyful noise unto him with psalms.

3 For the Lord is a great God, and a great King above all gods.

4 In his hand are the deep places of the earth: the strength of the hills is his also.

5 The sea is his, and he made it: and his hands formed the dry land.

6 O come, let us worship and bow down: let us kneel before the Lord our maker.

7 For he is our God, and we are the people of his pasture, and the sheep of his hand: to day if ye will hear his voice.

8 Harden not your heart, as in the provocation, and as in the day of temptation in the wilderness.

9 When your fathers tempted me, proved me, and saw my work.

10 Forty years long was I grieved with this generation, and said, It is a people that do err in their heart, and they have not known my ways.

11 Unto whom I sware in my wrath, that they should not enter into my rest.

PSALM XCVI.

O Sing unto the Lord a new song: sing unto the Lord all the earth.

2 Sing unto the Lord, bless his name: shew forth his salvation from day to day.

3 Declare his glory among the heathen, his wonders a-

mong all people.

4 For the Lord is great, and greatly to be praised: he is to be feared above all gods.

5 For all the gods of the nations are idols: but the Lord made the heavens.

6 Honour and majesty are before him: strength and beauty are in his sanctuary.

7 Give unto the Lord, O ye kindreds of the people, give unto the Lord glory and strength.

8 Give unto the Lord the glory due unto his name: bring an offering and come into his courts.

9 O worship the Lord in the beauty of holiness: fear before him all the earth.

10 Say among the heathen, that the Lord reigneth: the world also shall be established that it shall not be moved; he shall judge the people righteously.

11 Let the heavens rejoice, and let the earth be glad: let the sea rore, and the fulness thereof.

12 Let the field be joyful, and all that is therein: then shall all the trees of the wood rejoice.

13 Before the Lord, for he cometh, for he cometh to judge the earth: he shall judge the world with righteousness, and the people with his truth.

PSALM XCVII.

THE Lord reigneth, let the earth rejoice: let the multitude of isles be glad thereof.

2. Clouds and darkness are round about him: righteousness and judgment are the habitation of his throne.

3 A fire goeth before him, and burneth up his enemies round about.

4 His lightnings enlightned the world: the earth saw and trembled.

5 The hills melted like wax at the presence of the Lord: at the presence of the Lord of the whole earth.

6 The heavens declare his righteousness: and all the people see his glory.

7 Confounded be all they that serve graven images, that boast themselves of idols: worship him, all ye gods.

8 Zion heard, and was glad, and the daughters of Judah rejoiced; because of thy judgments, O Lord.

9 For thou, Lord, art high above all the earth: thou ar exalted far above all gods.

10 Ye that love the Lord, hat evil: he preserveth the souls o his saints, he delivereth then out of the hand of the wicked

11 Light is sown for th righteous, and gladness for th upright in heart.

12 Rejoice in the Lord, ye righ teous: and give thanks at th remembrance of his holiness.

: XCVIII.
the Lord a
for he hath
s things : his
his holy arm
the victory.
l hath made
tion : his righ-
e openly shew-
of the heathen.
emembered his
uth toward the
all the ends of
een the salvati-

yful noise unto
e earth : make
d rejoice and

the Lord with
the harp, and
salm.
pets, and sound
e a joyful noise
, the King.
roar, and the
the world, and
therein.
oods clap their
hills be joyful

Lord; for he
ge the earth :
ness shall he
l, and the peo-

M XCIX.
d reigneth, let
ople tremble :
een the cheru-
arth be moved.

2 The Lord is great in Zion, and he is high above all people.

3 Let them praise thy great and terrible name, for it is holy.

4 The king's strength also loveth judgment : thou dost establish equity, thou executest judgment and righteousness in Jacob.

5 Exalt ye the Lord our God, and worship at his footstool, for he is holy.

6 Moses and Aaron among his priests, and Samuel among them that call upon his name : they called upon the Lord, and he answered them.

7 He spake unto them in the cloudy pillar; they kept his testimonies, and the ordinance that he gave them.

8 Thou answeredst them, O Lord our God : thou wast a God that forgavest them, though thou tookest vengeance of their inventions.

9 Exalt the Lord our God, and worship at his holy hill; for the Lord our God is holy.

PSALM C.

MAke a joyful noise unto the Lord, all ye lands.

2 Serve the Lord with gladness : come before his presence with singing.

3 Know ye that the Lord he is God, it is he that hath made us, and not we ourselves : we are his people, and the

sheep of his pasture.

4. Enter into his gates with thanksgiving, and into his courts with praise: be thankful unto him, and bless his name.

5 For the Lord is good, his mercy is everlasting: and his truth endureth to all generations.

PSALM CI.

I Will sing of mercy and judgment, unto thee, O Lord, will I sing.

2 I will behave myself wisely in a perfect way: O when wilt thou come unto me? I will walk within my house with a perfect heart.

3 I will set no wicked thing before mine eyes: I hate the work of them that turned aside, it shall not cleave to me.

4. A froward heart shall depart from me. I will not know a wicked person.

5 Whoso privily slandereth his neighbour, him will I cut off: him that hath an high look, and a proud heart, will not I suffer.

6 Mine eyes shall be upon the faithful of the land, that they may dwell with me: he that walketh in a perfect way, he shall serve me.

7 He that worketh deceit, shall not dwell within my house: he that telleth lies, shall not tarry in my sight.

8 I will early destroy all the wicked of the land: that I may cut off all wicthe city of th

PSA

Hear my
    and let
unto thee.

2 Hide no
me, in the da
trouble, incli
me: in the
answer me spe

3 For my
ed like smoke
are burnt as a

4 My hea
withered like
forget to eat

5 By reaso
my groaning
to my skin.

6 I am lik
wilderness, I
of the desart.

7 I watch,
row alone up

8 Mine e
me all the da
are mad agai
against me.

9 For I hav
bread, and m
with weeping

10 Because
nation and
thou hast lifte
me down.

11 My da
dow that decl
withered like

12 But tho
endure for ev

25 Of old hast thou laid the foundation of the earth; and the heavens are the work of thy hands.

26 They shall perish, but thou shalt endure; yea, all of them shall wax old like a garment; as a vesture shalt thou change them, and they shall be changed.

27 But thou art the same, and thy years shall have no end.

28 The children of thy servants shall continue, and their seed shall be established before thee.

PSALM CIII.

Bless the Lord, O my soul; and all that is within me, bless his holy name.

2 Bless the Lord, O my soul, and forget not all his benefits.

3 Who forgiveth all thine iniquities: who healeth all thy diseases.

4 Who redeemeth thy life from destruction; who crowneth thee with loving kindness and tender mercies.

5 Who satisfieth thy mouth with good things: so that thy youth is renewed like the eagles.

6 The Lord executeth righteousness and judgment for all that are oppressed.

7 He made known his ways unto Moses, his acts unto the children of Israel.

8 The Lord is merciful and

gracious, flow to anger, and plenteous in mercy.

9 He will not always chide; neither will he keep his anger for ever.

10 He hath not dealt with us after our sins; nor rewarded us according to our iniquities.

11 For as the heaven is high above the earth: so great is his mercy toward them that fear him.

12 As far as the east is from the west, so far hath he removed our transgressions from us.

13 Like as a father pitieth his children: so the Lord pitieth them that fear him.

14 For he knoweth our frame: he remembereth that we are dust.

15 As for a man, his days are as grass: as a flower of the field, so he flourisheth.

16 For the wind passeth over it, and it is gone, and the place thereof shall know it no more.

17 But the mercy of the Lord is from everlasting to everlasting upon them that fear him: and his righteousness unto childrens children.

18 To such as keep his covenant, and to those that remember his commandments to do them.

19 The Lord hath prepared his throne in the heavens; and his kingdom ruleth over all.

20 Bless the Lord, ye his angels that excel in strength, that do his commandments, hearkening unto the voice of his word.

21 Bless ye the Lord, all ye his hosts, ye ministers of his that do his pleasure.

22 Bless the Lord, all his works, in all places of his dominion: bless the Lord, O my soul.

PSALM CIV.

BLess the Lord, O my Soul: O Lord my God, thou art very great, thou art cloathed with honour and majesty.

2 Who coverest thyself with light, as with a garment; who stretchest out the heavens like a curtain.

3 Who layeth the beams of his chambers in the waters, who maketh the clouds his chariot, who walketh upon the wings of the wind.

4 Who maketh his angels spirits, his ministers a flaming fire.

5 Who laid the foundations of the earth, that it should not be removed for ever.

6 Thou coverest it with the deep, as with a garment; the water stood above the mountains.

7 At thy rebuke they fled; at the voice of thy thunder they hasted away.

8 They go up by the mountains: they go down by the vallies unto the place which

d for them.
ſet a bound
ot paſs over:
not again to

h the ſprings
which run a-

drink to ev-
eld; the wild
r thirſt.
hall the fowls
ve their habi-
ng among the

eth the hills
rs: the earth
he fruit of thy

the graſs to
le, and herb
man; that he
food out of

that maketh
man, and oil
to ſhine, and
gtheneſt mans

of the Lord are
cedars of Leb-
th planted.
e birds make
for the ſtork,
er houſe.
re a refuge for
and the rocks

ted the moon
ſun knoweth

20 Thou makeſt darkneſs, and it is night: wherein all the beaſts of the foreſt do creep forth.

21 The young lions roar after their prey, and ſeek their meat from God.

22 The ſun ariſeth, they gather themſelves together; and lay them down in their dens.

23 Men goeth forth to his work, and to his labour until the evening.

24 O Lord, how manifold are thy works! in wiſdom haſt thou made them all: the earth is full of thy riches.

25 So is this great and wide ſea, wherein are things creeping innumerable, both ſmall and great beaſts.

26 There go the ſhips: there is that leviathan whom thou haſt made to play therein.

27 Theſe wait all upon thee: that thou mayeſt give them their meat in due ſeaſon.

28 That thou giveſt them they gather: thou openeſt thine hand, they are filled with good.

29 Thou hideſt thy face, they are troubled: thou takeſt away their breath, they die, and return to their duſt.

30 Thou ſendeſt forth thy ſpirit, they are created: and thou reneweſt the face of the earth.

31 The glory of the Lord ſhall endure for ever; the Lord ſhall rejoice in his works.

32 He looketh on the earth, and it trembleth: he toucheth

the hills, and they smoke.

33 I will sing unto the lord as long as I live: I will sing praise unto my God, while I have my being.

34 My meditation of him shall be sweet; I will be glad in the Lord.

35 Let the sinners be consumed out of the earth, and let the wicked be no more: bless thou the Lord, O my soul. Praise ye the Lord.

PSALM CV.

O Give thanks unto the Lord: call upon his name: make known his deeds among the people.

2 Sing unto him, sing psalms unto him: talk ye of all his wondrous works.

3 Glory ye in his holy name, let the heart of them rejoice that seek the Lord.

4 Seek the Lord, and his strength: seek his face evermore.

5 Remember his marvellous works that he hath done; his wonders and the judgments of his mouth.

6 O ye seed of Abraham his servant, ye children of Jacob his chosen.

7 He is the Lord our God, his judgments are in all the earth.

8 He hath remembered his covenant for ever; the word which he commanded to a thousand generations.

9 Which covenant he made with Abraham, and his oath unto Isaac.

10 And confi[rmed] to Jacob for [a] rael for an eve[r]

11 Saying, I give the lan[d] lot of your inh[eritance]

12 When few men in n[umber] ry few, and st[rangers]

13 When one nation to a[nother] kingdom to a[nother]

14 He suf[fered] do them wron[g] proved kings

15 Saying, anointed, and no harm.

16 Moreov[er] a famine upo[n] break the who[le]

17 He sen[t] them, even J[oseph] sold for a serv[ant]

18 Whose fe[et] fetters; he wa[s]

19 Until t[he] word came: Lord tried hi[m]

20 The kin[g] him: even t[he] people, and l[et]

21 He mad[e] house, and ru[ler] stance:

22 To bin[d] his pleasure: senators wisdo[m]

23 Israel [came into E]gypt: and Ja[cob]

the land of Ham.

24 And he increased his people greatly: and made them stronger than their enemies.

25 He turned their heart to hate his people, to deal subtilly with his servants.

26 He sent Moses his servant, & Aaron whom he had chosen.

27 They shewed his signs among them, and wonders in the land of Ham.

28 He sent darkness, and made it dark: and they rebelled not against his word.

29 He turned their waters into blood, and slew their fish.

30 Their land brought forth frogs in abundance, in the chambers of their kings.

31 He spake, and there came divers sorts of flies, and lice in all their coasts.

32 He gave them hail for rain: and flaming fire in their land.

33 He smote their vines also and their fig-trees; and break the trees of their coasts.

34 He spake and the locusts came; and caterpillars, and that without number.

35 And did eat up all the herbs in their land: and devoured the fruit of their ground.

36 He smote also all the first-born in their land: the chief of all their strength.

37 He brought them forth also with silver and gold: and there was not one feeble person among their tribes.

38 Egypt was glad when they departed; for the fear of them fell upon them.

39 He spread a cloud for a covering, and fire to give light in the night.

40 The people asked, and he brought quails; and satisfied them with the bread of heaven.

41 He opened the rock, and the waters gushed out, they ran in the dry places like a river.

42 For he remembered his holy promise, and Abraham his servant.

43 And he brought forth his people with joy, and his chosen with gladness.

44 And gave them the lands of the heathen: and they inherited the labour of the people.

45 That they might observe his statutes, and keep his laws. Praise ye the Lord.

PSALM CVI.

PRaise ye the Lord, O give thanks unto the Lord, for he is good, for his mercy endureth for ever.

2 Who can utter the mighty acts of the Lord? who can shew forth all his praise?

3 Blessed are they that keep judgment; and he that doth righteousness at all times.

4 Remember me, O Lord, with the favour that thou bearest unto thy people: O visit me with thy salvation.

5 That I may see the good

of thy chosen, that I may rejoice in the gladness of thy nation: that I may glory with thine inheritance.

6 We have sinned with our fathers: we have committed iniquity; we have done wickedly.

7 Our fathers understood not thy wonders in Egypt, they remembered not the multitude of thy mercies; but provoked him at the sea, even at the red sea.

8 Nevertheless, he saved them for his names sake: that he might make his mighty power to be known.

9 He rebuked the red sea also, and it was dried up: so he led them through the depths as through the wilderness.

10 And he saved them from the hand of him that hated them: and redeemed them from the hand of the enemy.

11 And the waters covered their enemeis; there was not one of them left.

12 Then believed they his words, they sang his praise.

13 They soon forgat his works, they waited not for his counsel.

14 But lusted exceedingly in the wilderness, and tempted God in the desart.

15 And he gave them their request, but sent leanness into their soul.

16 They envied Moses also in the camp, and Aaron the saint of the Lord.

17 The earth opened and swallowed up Dathan, and covered the company of Abiram.

18 And a fire was kindled in their company; and the flame burnt up the wicked.

19 They made a calf in Horeb, and worshipped the molten image.

20 Thus they changed their glory into the similitude of an ox that eateth grass.

21 They forgat God the saviour, which had done great things in Egypt:

22 Wondrous works in the land of Ham, and terrible things by the red sea.

23 Therefore he said that he would destroy them, had not Moses his chosen stood before him in the breach, to turn away his wrath, lest he should destroy them.

24 Yea they despised the pleasant land: they believed not his word.

25 But murmured in their tents, and hearkened not unto the voice of the Lord.

26 Therefore he lifted up his hand against them, to overthrow them in the wilderness

27 To overthrow their seed also among the nations, and to scatter them in the lands.

28 They joined themselves also unto baal-peor, and ate the sacrifices of the dead.

29 Thus they provoked him to anger with their inventions,

they that hated them, ruled over them.

42 Their enemies also oppressed them, and they were brought into subjection under their hand.

43 Many times did he deliver them, but they provoked him with their counsel, and were brought low for their iniquity.

44 Nevertheless, he regarded their affliction, when he heard their cry.

45 And he remembered for them his covenant, and repented according to the multitude of his mercies.

46 He made them also to be pitied of all those that carried them captives.

47 Save us, O Lord our God, and gather us from among the heathen, to give thanks unto thy holy name, and to triumph in thy praise.

48 Blessed be the Lord God of Israel, from everlasting to everlasting; & let all the people say Amen. Praise ye the Lord.

PSALM CVII.

O Give thanks unto the Lord, for he is good for his mercy endureth for ever.

2 Let the redeemed of the Lord say so, whom he hath redeemed from the hand of the enemy.

3 And gathered them out of the lands, from the east and from the west, from the north and from the south.

4 They wandred in the wilderness in a solitary way, they found no city to dwell in.

5 Hungry and thirsty, their soul fainted in them.

6 Then they cried unto the Lord in their trouble, and he delivered them out of their distresses.

7 And he led them forth by the right way, that they might go to a city of habitation.

8 O that men would praise the Lord for his goodness, and for his wonderful works to the children of men!

9 For he satisfieth the longing soul, and filleth the hungry soul with goodness.

10 Such as sit in darkness and in the shadow of death, being bound in affliction and iron.

11 Because they rebelled against the words of God, and contemned the counsel of the most high.

12 Therefore he brought down their heart with labour, they fell down, and there was none to help.

13 Then they cried unto the Lord in their trouble, & he saved them out of their distresses.

14 He brought them out of darkness and the shadow of death: and break their bands in sunder.

15 O that men would praise the Lord for his goodness, and for his wonderful works to the

16 For he hath broken the gates of brass, and cut the b[ars] of iron in sunder.

17 Fools, because of th[eir] transgression, and because their iniquities, are afflicted.

18 Their soul abhorreth manner of meat, and they dr[aw] near unto the gates of death.

19 Then they cry unto Lord in their trouble, he sav[ed] them out of their distresses.

20 He sent his word a[nd] healed them, and delive[red] them from their destructions.

21 O that Men would pr[aise] the Lord for his goodness, [and] for his wonderful works to children of men.

22 And let them sacrifice sacrifices of thanksgiving, & [de]clare his works with rejoici[ng]

23 They that go down [to] the sea in ships, that do b[usi]ness in great waters:

24 These see the works the Lord, and his wonder[s in] the deep.

25 For he commandeth [and] raiseth the stormy wind, w[hich] lifteth up the waves thereof

26 They mount up to heaven, they go down aga[in to] the depths; their soul is me[lted] because of trouble.

27 They reel to and [fro,] and stagger like a drun[ken] man, and are at their wits[' end.]

28 Then they cry unto [the] Lord in their trouble, an[d]

ſies.

29 He maketh the ſtorm a [calm], ſo that the waters there[of] are ſtill.

30 Then are they glad be[cau]ſe they be quiet: ſo he bring[eth] them unto their deſired [ha]ven.

31 O that men would praiſe [the] Lord for his goodneſs, and [for] his wonderful works to the [chi]ldren of men!

32 Let them exalt him alſo [in] the congregation of the peo[ple], and praiſe him in the aſ[ſem]bly of the elders.

33 He turneth rivers into a [wil]derneſs, and the water[ſpr]ings into dry ground:

34 A fruitful land into bar[ren]neſs, for the wickedneſs of [th]em that dwell therein.

35 He turneth the wilder[neſ]s into a ſtanding water, and [dry] ground into water ſprings.

36 And there he maketh the [hu]ngry to dwell, that they may [pre]pare a city for habitation;

37 And ſow the fields and [pla]nt vineyards; which may [yie]ld fruits of increaſe.

38 He bleſſeth them alſo, ſo [tha]t they are multiplied great[ly], and ſuffereth not their cat[tle] to decreaſe.

where there is no way.

41 Yet ſetteth he the poor on high from afflction, and maketh him families like a flock.

42 The righteous ſhall ſee it and rejoice; and all iniquity ſhall ſtop her mouth.

43 Whoſo is wiſe, and will obſerve thoſe things, even they ſhall underſtand the loving kindneſs of the Lord.

PSALM CVIII.

O God, my heart is fixed, I will ſing and give praiſe, even with my glory.

2 Awake pſaltery and harp, I myſelf will awake early.

3 I will praiſe thee, O Lord, among the people: and I will ſing praiſes unto thee among the nations.

4 For thy mercy is great above the heavens, and thy truth reacheth unto the clouds.

5 Be thou exalted, O God, above the heavens, and thy glory above all the earth.

6 That thy beloved may be delivered: ſave with thy right hand, and anſwer me.

7 God hath ſpoken in his holineſs, I will rejoice, I will divide Shechem, and meet out the valley of Succoth.

8 Gilead is mine, Manaſſeh

10 Who will bring me into the strong city? who will lead me into Edom?

11 Wilt not thou, O God, who hast cast us off? and wilt not thou, O God, go forth with our hosts?

12 Give us help from trouble, for vain is the help of man.

13 Through God we shall do valiantly, for he it is that shall tread down our enemies.

PSALM CIX.

Hold not thy peace, O God of my praise.

2 For the mouth of the wicked, and the mouth of the deceitful are opened against me, they have spoken against me with a lying tongue.

3 They compassed me about also with words of hatred, and fought against me without a cause.

4 For my love they are my adversaries: but I give myself unto prayer.

5 And they have rewarded me evil for good, and hatred for my love.

6 Set thou a wicked man over him; and let Satan stand at his right hand.

7 When he shall be judged, let him be condemned: and

tinually vaga
let them see
out of the de

11 Let th
all that he l
stranger spoi

12 Let th
tend mercy
let there be
fatherless chi

13 Let his
and in the ge
let their nam

14 Let t
fathers be
the Lord: a
of his mothe

15 Let t
Lord contin
cut off the
from the ear

16 Becau
bered not t
persecuted t
man, that l
the broken

17 As he
let it come u
lighted not
be far from

18 As h
with cursin
garment;
his bowels l
oil into his

m that speak
ul.
u for me, O
or thy names
hy mercy is
u me.
or & needy, &
ed within me.
like the sha-
lineth : I am
n as the locust.
are weak
and my flesh

reproach un-
ey looked up-
d their heads.
O Lord my
, according

may know
nd, that thou

arse, but bless
ey arise, let
; but let thy

idversaries be
ne, & let them
with their own
a mantle.
praise the Lord
ea, I will praise
nultitude.
I stand at the
 poor, to save
hat condemn

CX.
aid unto my
 thou at my

right hand, until I make thine enemies thy foot-stool.

2 The Lord shall send the rod of thy strength out of Zion : rule thou in the midst of thine enemies.

3 Thy people shall be willing in the day of thy power, in the beauties of holiness, from the womb of the morning : thou hast the dew of thy youth.

4 The Lord hath sworn and will not repent, Thou art a priest for ever, after the order of Melchisedec.

5 The Lord at thy right hand shall strike through kings in the day of his wrath.

6 He shall judge among the heathen, he shall fill the places with the dead bodies : he shall wound the heads over many countries.

7 He shall drink of the brook in the way : therefore shall he lift up the head.

PSALM CXI.

PRaise ye the Lord ; I will praise the Lord with my whole heart, in the assembly of the upright, and in the congregation.

2 The works of the Lord are great, sought out of all them that have pleasure therein.

3 His work is honourable and glorious: and his righteousness endureth for ever.

4 He hath made his wonderful works to be remembered ; the Lord is gracious and full

of compassion.

5 He hath given meat unto them that fear him: he will ever be mindful of his covenant.

6 He hath shewed his people the power of his works, that he may give them the heritage of the heathen.

7 The works of his hands are verity and judgment: all his commandments are sure.

8 They stand fast for ever and ever, and are done in truth and uprightness.

9 He sent redemption unto his people: he hath commanded his covenant for ever: holy and reverend is his name.

10 The fear of the Lord is the beginning of wisdom: a good understanding have all they that do his commandments: his praise endureth for ever.

PSALM CXII.

Praise ye the Lord. Blessed is the man that feareth the Lord, that delighteth greatly in his commandments.

2 His seed shall be mighty upon earth: the generation of the upright shall be blessed.

3 Wealth and riches shall be in his house: and his righteousness endureth for ever.

4 Unto the upright there ariseth light in the darkness: he is gracious, and full of compassion, and righteous.

5 A good man sheweth favour and lendeth: he will guide his affairs with discretion.

6 Surely he shall not be moved for ever: the righteous shall be in everlasting remembrance.

7 He shall not be afraid of evil tidings: his heart is fixed, trusting in the Lord.

8 His heart is established, he shall not be afraid, until he see his desire upon his enemies.

9 He hath dispersed, he hath given to the poor: his righteousness endureth for ever: his horn shall be exalted with honour.

10 The wicked shall see it, & be grieved: he shall gnash with his teeth, & melt away: the desire of the wicked shall perish.

PSALM CXIII.

Praise ye the Lord. Praise, O ye servants of the Lord, praise the name of the Lord.

2 Blessed be the name of the Lord from this time forth and for ever more.

3 From the rising of the sun, unto the going down of the same, the Lord's name is to be praised.

4 The Lord is high above all nations, and his glory above the heavens.

5 Who is like unto the Lord our God, who dwelleth on high!

6 Who humbleth himself to behold the things that are in heaven, and in the earth.

7 He raiseth up the poor out of the dust, and lifteth the

[EW-ENGLAND PSALTER.

dunghill.
y fet him with
th the princes

ι the barren
ιoufe, and to
er of children.
·d.

CXIV.

el went out of
the houfe of
ople of ftrange

his fanctuary,
ninion.
w it and fled;
en back.
tains fkipped
the little hills

ee, O thou fea,
? thou Jordan,
iven back?
ins, that ye
s; and ye lit-
bs?
hou earth, at
e lord, at the
od of Jacob.
ned the rock
ater, the flint
f waters.

CXV.

us, O Lord,
us, but unto
glory, for thy
y truth fake.
hould the hea-
is now their

d i in the hea

vens, he hath done whatfoever he pleafed.

4 Their idols are filver and gold, the work of mens hands.

5 They have mouths, but they fpeak not; eyes have they but they fee not.

6 They have ears, but they hear not: nofes have they, but they fmell not.

7 They have hands, but they handle not; feet have they, but they walk not: neither fpeak they through their throat.

8 They that make them are like unto them; fo is every one that trufteth in them.

9 O Ifrael, truft thou in the Lord; he is their help and their fhield.

10 O houfe of Aaron, truft in the Lord: he is their help and their fhield.

11 Ye that fear the Lord, truft in the Lord, he is their help and their fhield.

12 The Lord hath been mindful of us, he will blefs us, he will blefs the houfe of Ifrael, he will blefs the houfe of Aaron.

13 He will blefs them that fear the Lord, both fmall and great.

14 The Lord fhall increafe you more and more, you and your children.

15 You are bleffed of the Lord which made heaven and earth.

16 The heaven, even the heavens are the Lord's: but the earth hath he given to the children of men.

17 The dead praise not the Lord, neither any that go down, into silence.

18 But he will bless the Lord, from this time forth and for evermore. Praise the Lord.

PSALM CXVI.

I Love the Lord because he hath heard my voice, and my supplications.

2 Because he hath inclined his ear unto me, therefore will I call upon him as long as I live.

3 The sorrows of death compassed me, and the pains of hell gat hold upon me: I found trouble and sorrow.

4 Then called I upon the name of the Lord: O Lord, I beseech thee deliver my soul.

5 Gracious is the Lord, and righteous: yea, our God is merciful.

6 The Lord preserveth the simple; I was brought low and he helped me.

7 Return unto thy rest, O my soul, for the Lord hath dealt bountifully with thee.

8 For thou hast delivered my soul from death, mine eyes from tears, and my feet from falling.

9 I will walk before the Lord in the land of the living.

10 I believed, therefore have I spoken: I was greatly afflicted.

11 I said in my haste, all men are liars.

12 What shall I render unto the Lord, for all his benefits towards me?

13 I will take the cup of salvation, and call upon the name of the Lord.

14 I will pay my vows unto the Lord, now in the presence of all his people.

15 Precious in the sight of the Lord is the death of his saints.

16 O Lord, truly I am thy servant, I am thy servant, and the son of thy handmaid, thou hast loosed my bonds.

17 I will offer to thee the sacrifice of thanksgiving, and will call upon the name of the Lord.

18 I will pay my vows unto the Lord, now in the presence of all his people.

19 In the courts of the Lord's house, in the midst of thee, O Jerusalem. Praise ye the Lord.

PSALM CXVII.

O Praise the Lord all ye nations: praise him all ye people.

2 For his merciful kindness is great towards us, and the truth of the Lord endureth for ever. Praise ye the Lord.

PSALM CXVIII.

O Give thanks unto the Lord, for he is good: because his mercy endureth for ever.

2 Let Israel now say, that his mercy endureth for ever.

3 Let the house of Aaron now say, that his mercy endureth for ever.

4 Let them now that fear the Lord, say that his mercy

endureth forever.

5 I call upon the Lord in distress; the Lord answered me, and set me in a large place.

6 The Lord is on my side, I will not fear: what can man do unto me?

7 The Lord taketh my part with them that help me: therefore shall I see my desire upon them that hate me.

8 It is better to trust in the Lord, than to put confidence in man.

9 It is better to trust in the Lord, than to put confidence in princes.

10 All nations compassed me about, but in the name of the Lord will I destroy them.

11 They compassed me about, yea, they compassed me about, but in the name of the Lord I will destroy them.

12 They compassed me about like bees, they are quenched as the fire of thorns: for in the name of the Lord I will destroy them.

13 Thou hast thrust sore at me that I might fall; but the Lord helped me.

14 The Lord is my strength & song, & is become my salvation.

15 The voice of rejoiceing & salvation is in the tabernacles of the righteous: the right hand of the Lord doeth valiantly.

16 The right hand of the Lord is exalted: the right hand of the Lord doeth valiantly.

17 I shall not die, but live, and declare the works of the Lord.

18 The Lord hath chastned me sore; but he hath not given me over unto death.

19 Open to me the gates of righteousness: I will go into them, and I will praise the Lord.

20 This gate of the Lord, into which the righteous shall enter.

21 I will praise thee, for thou hast heard me, and art become my salvation.

22 The stone which the builders refused, is become the head stone of the corner.

23 This is the Lord's doing, it is marvellous in our eyes.

24 This is the day which the Lord hath made, we will rejoice and be glad in it.

25 Save now I beseech thee O Lord: O Lord, I beseech thee, send now prosperity.

26 Blessed be he that cometh in the name of the Lord, we have blessed you out of the house of the Lord.

27 God is the Lord which hath shewed us light; bind the sacrifice with cords, even unto the horns of the altar.

28 Thou art my God, and I will praise thee, thou art my God, I will exalt thee.

29 O give thanks unto the Lord, for he is good: for his mercy endureth for ever.

PSALM CXIX.
ALEPH.

Blessed are the undefiled in the way, who walk in

the law of the Lord.

2 Blessed are they that keep his testimonies, and that seek him with the whole heart.

3 They also do no iniquity: they walk in his ways.

4 Thou hast commanded us to keep thy precepts diligently.

5 O that my ways were directed to keep thy statutes.

6 Then shall I not be ashamed, when I have respect unto all thy commandments.

7 I will praise thee with uprightness of heart, when I shall have learned thy righteous judgments.

8 I will keep thy statutes: O forsake me not utterly.

BETH.

9 Wherewith shall a young man cleanse his way? by taking heed thereto according to thy word.

10 With my whole heart have I sought thee: O let me not wander from thy commandments.

11 Thy word have I hid in mine heart, that I might not sin against thee.

12 Blessed art thou, O Lord: teach me thy statutes.

13 With my lips have I declared all the judgments of thy mouth.

14 I have rejoiced in the way of thy testimonies, as much as in all riches.

15 I will meditate in thy precepts, and have respect unto thy ways.

16 I will delight myself in thy statutes: I will not forgive thy word.

GIMEL.

17 Deal bountifully with thy servant, that I may live and keep thy word.

18 Open thou mine eyes, that I may behold wondrous things out of thy law.

19 I am a stranger in the earth; hide not thy commandments from me.

20 My soul breaketh for the longing that it hath unto thy judgments at all times.

21 Thou hast rebuked the proud that are cursed, which do err from thy commandments.

22 Remove from me reproach and contempt, for I have kept thy testimonies.

23 Princes also did sit & speak against me: but thy servant did meditate in thy statutes.

24 Thy testimonies also are my delight, and my counsellors.

DALETH.

25 My soul cleaveth unto the dust; quicken thou me according to thy word.

26 I have declared my ways, and thou heardest me. Teach me thy statutes.

27 Make me to understand the way of thy precepts: so shall I talk of thy wondrous works.

28 My soul melteth for heaviness; strengthen thou me according unto thy word.

29 Remove from me the way of lying, and grant me thy law graciously.

30 I have chosen the way of truth: thy judgments have I laid before me.

31 I have stuck unto thy testimonies; O Lord, put me not to shame.

32 I will run the way of thy commandments, when thou shalt enlarge my heart.

HE.

33 Teach me, O Lord, the way of thy statutes, and I shall keep it unto the end.

34 Give me understanding, and I shall keep thy law: yea, I shall observe it with my whole heart.

35 Make me to go in the path of thy commandments: for therein do I delight.

36 Incline my heart unto thy testimonies, and not to covetousness.

37 Turn away mine eyes from beholding vanity: and quicken thou me in thy way.

38 Stablish thy word unto thy servant, who is devoted to thy fear.

39 Turn away my reproach which I fear, for thy judgments are good.

40 Behold I have longed after thy precepts: quicken me in thy righteousness.

VAU.

41 Let thy mercies come also unto me, O Lord: even thy salvation, according to thy word.

42 So shall I have wherewith to answer him that reproacheth me: for I trust in thy word.

43 And take not the word of truth utterly out of my mouth; for I have hoped in thy judgments.

44 So shall I keep thy law continually for ever and ever.

45 And I will walk at liberty; for I seek thy precepts.

46 I will speak of thy testimonies also before kings, and will not be ashamed.

47 And I will delight myself in thy commandments, which I have loved.

48 My hands also will I lift up unto thy commandments, which I have loved: and I will meditate in thy statutes.

ZAIN.

49 Remember the word unto thy servant, upon which thou hast caused me to hope.

50 This is my comfort in my affliction; for thy word hath quickened me.

51 The proud have had me greatly in derision: yet have I not declined from thy law.

52 I remembered thy judgments of old, O Lord, and have comforted myself.

53 Horror hath taken hold upon me, because of the wicked that forsake thy law.

54 Thy statutes have been my songs in the house of my

pilgrimage.

55 I have remembred thy name, O Lord, in the night, and have kept thy law.

56 This I had, becauſe I kept thy precepts.

CHETH.

57 Thou art my portion, O Lord, I have ſaid, that I would keep thy words.

58 I intreated thy favour with my whole heart: be merciful unto me, according to thy word.

59 I thought on my ways, and turned my feet unto thy teſtimonies.

60 I made haſte, and delayed not to keep thy commandments.

61 The bands of the wicked have robbed me; but I have not forgotten thy law.

62 At midnight I will riſe to give thanks unto thee; becauſe of thy righteous judgments.

63 I am a companion of all them that fear thee, and of them that keep thy precepts.

64 The earth, O Lord, is full of thy mercy: teach me thy ſtatutes.

TETH.

65 Thou haſt dealt well with thy ſervant, O Lord, according unto thy word.

66 Thou art good and doeſt good: teach me thy ſtatutes.

69 The proud have forged a lie againſt me: but I will keep thy precepts with my whole heart.

70 Their heart is as fat as greaſe: but I delighted in thy law.

71 It is good for me that I have been afflicted: that I might learn thy ſtatutes.

72 The law of thy mouth is better unto me than thouſands of gold and ſilver.

JOD.

73 Thy hands have made me and faſhioned me: give me underſtanding, that I may learn thy commandments.

74 They that fear thee will be glad when they ſee me: becauſe I have hoped in thy word.

75 I know, O Lord, that thy judgments are right, and that thou in faithfulneſs haſt afflicted me.

76 Let, I pray thee, thy merciful kindneſs be for my comfort, according to thy word unto thy ſervant.

77 Let thy tender mercies come unto me, that I may live: for thy law is my delight.

78 Let the proud be aſham-

80 Let my heart be found in thy statutes, that I be not ashamed.

81 My soul fainteth for thy salvation: but I hope in thy word.

82 Mine eyes fail for thy word saying, when wilt thou comfort me?

83 For I am become like a bottle in the smoke: yet do I not forget thy statutes.

84 How many are the days of thy servant? when wilt thou execute judgment on them that persecute me?

85 The proud have digged pits for me, which are not after thy law.

86 All thy commandments are faithful: they persecute me wrongfully; help thou me.

87 They had almost consumed me upon earth: but I forsook not thy precepts.

88 Quicken me after thy loving kindness: so shall I keep the testimony of thy mouth.

LAMED.

89 For ever, O Lord, thy word is settled in heaven.

90 Thy faithfulness is unto all generations; thou hast established the earth, and it abideth.

91 They continue this day according to thine ordinances: for all are thy servants.

92 Unless thy law had been my delight, I should then have perished in mine affliction.

93 I will never forget thy precepts: for with them thou hast quickned me.

94 I am thine, save me: for I have sought thy precepts.

95 The wicked have waited for me to destroy me: but I will consider thy testimonies.

96 I have seen an end of all perfection: but thy commandment is exceeding broad.

MEM.

97 Oh how love I thy law! it is my meditation all the day.

98 Thou through thy commandments hast made me wiser than mine enemies: for they are ever with me.

99 I have more understanding than all my teachers: for thy testimonies are my meditation.

100 I understand more than the ancients: because I keep thy precepts.

101 I have refrained my feet from every evil way: that I might keep thy word.

102 I have not departed from thy judgments: for thou hast taught me.

103 How sweet are thy words unto my taste! yea, sweeter than honey to my mouth.

104 Through thy precepts I get understanding; therefore I hate every false way.

NUN.

105 Thy word is a lamp unto my feet, and a light unto my path.

106 I have sworn, and I will

perform it, that I will keep thy righteous judgments.

107 I am afflicted very much; quicken me, O Lord, according unto thy word.

108 Accept, I beseech thee, the free-will offerings of my mouth, O Lord, and teach me thy judgments.

109 My soul is continually in my hand, yet do I not forget thy law.

110 The wicked have laid a snare for me: yet I erred not from thy precepts.

111 Thy testimonies have I taken as an heritage for ever: for they are the rejoicing of my heart.

112 I have inclined my heart to perform thy statutes alway, even unto the end.

SAMECH.

113 I hate vain thoughts, but thy law do I love.

114 Thou art my hiding place, and my shield: I hope in thy word.

115 Depart from me, ye evil doers: for I will keep the commandments of my God.

116 Uphold me according unto thy word, that I may live: and let me not be ashamed of my hope.

117 Hold thou me up, and I shall be safe: and I will have respect unto thy statutes continually.

118 Thou hast trodden down all them that err from thy statutes: for their deceit is falshood.

119 Thou puttest away all the wicked of the earth like dross: therefore I love thy testimonies.

120 My flesh trembleth for fear of thee, and I am afraid of thy judgments.

AIN.

121 I have done judgment and justice: leave me not to mine oppressors.

122 Be surety for thy servant for good; let not the proud oppress me.

123 Mine eyes fail for thy salvation, and for the word of thy righteousness.

124 Deal with thy servant according unto thy mercy, and teach me thy statutes.

125 I am thy servant, give me understanding; that I may know thy testimonies.

126 It is time for thee, Lord to work; for they have made void thy law.

127 Therefore I love thy commandments above gold, yea, above fine gold.

128 Therefore I esteem all thy precepts concerning all things to be right; and I hate every false way.

PE.

129 Thy testimonies are wonderful: therefore doth my soul keep them.

130 The entrance of thy words giveth light; it giveth

144 The righteousness of thy testimonies is everlasting: give me understanding, and I shall live.

KOPH.

145 I cried with my whole heart, hear me, O Lord: I will keep thy statutes.

146 I cried unto thee, save me, and I shall keep thy testimonies.

147 I prevented the dawning of the morning, and cried: I hoped in thy word.

148 Mine eyes prevent the night-watches, that I might meditate in thy word.

149 Hear my voice according unto thy loving-kindness: O Lord, quicken me according to thy judgment.

150 They draw nigh that follow after mischief: they are far from thy law.

151 Thou art near, O Lord: and all thy commandments are truth.

152 Concerning thy testimonies, I have known of old: that thou hast founded them for ever.

RESH.

153 Consider mine affliction and deliver me: for I do not forget thy law.

154 Plead my cause and deliver me: quicken me according to thy word.

155 Salvation is far from the wicked; for they seek not thy statutes.

G

156 Great

156 Great are thy tender mercies, O Lord: quicken me according to thy judgments.

157 Many are my persecutors, and mine enemies: yet do I not decline from thy testimonies.

158 I beheld the transgressors, and was grieved because they kept not thy word.

159 Consider how I love thy precepts: quicken me, O Lord, according to thy loving kindness.

160 Thy word is true from the beginning: and every one of thy righteous judgments endureth for ever.

SCHIN.

161 Princes have persecuted me without a cause: but my heart standeth in awe of thy word.

162 I rejoice at thy word as one that findeth great spoil.

163 I hate and abhor lying: but thy law do I love.

164 Seven times a day do I praise thee: because of thy righteous Judgments.

165 Great peace have they which love thy law: and nothing shall offend them.

166 Lord, I have hoped for thy salvation: and done thy commandments.

167 My soul hath kept thy testimonies; and I love them exceedingly.

168 I have kept thy precepts and thy testimonies; for all my ways are before thee.

TAU.

169 Let my cry come before thee, O Lord; give understanding according to word.

170 Let my supplica come before thee: delive according to thy word.

171 My lips shall praise, when thou hast ta me thy statutes.

172 My tongue shall s of thy word: for all thy mandments are righteousn

173 Let thine hand help for I have chosen thy prec

174 I have longed for salvation, O Lord: and law is my delight.

175 Let my soul live, it shall praise thee; and le judgments help me.

176 I have gone astray a lost sheep, seek thy serv for I do not forget thy mandments.

PSALM CXX.

IN my distress I cried unto Lord, and he heard m

2 Deliver my soul, O L from lying lips, and fr deceitful tongue.

3 What shall be given thee? or what shall be unto thee, thou false tong

4 Sharp arrows of the m ty, with coals of juniper.

5 Wo is me, that I soj in Mesech, that I dwell i tents of Kedar.

6 My soul hath long with him that hateth pea

7 I am for peace, but when I speak, they are for war.

PSALM CXXI.

I Will lift up mine eyes unto the hills, from whence cometh my help.

2 My help cometh from the Lord, which made heaven and earth.

3 He will not suffer thy foot to be moved: he that keepeth thee, will not slumber.

4 Behold, he that keepeth Israel, shall neither slumber nor sleep.

5 The Lord is thy keeper, the Lord is thy shade upon thy right hand.

6 The sun shall not smite thee by day, nor the moon by night.

7 The Lord shall preserve thee from all evil: he shall preserve thy soul.

8 The Lord shall preserve thy going out, and thy coming in, from this time forth, and even for ever more.

PSALM CXXII.

I Was glad when they said unto me, Let us go into the house of the Lord.

2 Our feet shall stand within thy gates, O Jerusalem.

3 Jerusalem is builded as a city that is compact together.

4 Whither the tribes go up, the tribes of the Lord, unto the testimony of Israel, to give thanks unto the name of the Lord.

5 For there are set thrones of judgment: the thrones of the house of David.

6 Pray for the peace of Jerusalem: they shall prosper that love thee.

7 Peace be within thy walls, & prosperity within thy palaces.

8 For my brethren and companions sakes, I will now say, Peace be within thee.

9 Because of the house of the Lord our God, I will seek thy good.

PSALM CXXIII.

UNto thee lift I up mine eyes: O thou that dwellest in the heavens.

2 Behold, as the eyes of servants look unto the hand of their masters, and as the eyes of the maiden unto the hand of her mistress: so our eyes wait upon the Lord our God, until that he have mercy upon us.

3 Have mercy upon us, O Lord, have mercy upon us; for we are exceedingly filled with contempt.

4 Our soul is exceedingly filled with the scorning of those that are at ease, and with the contempt of the proud.

PSALM CXXIV.

IF it had not been the Lord who was on our side, now may Israel say;

2 If it had not been the Lord who was on our side, when men rose up against us.

3 Then they had swallowed us up quick, when their wrath was kindled against us.

4 Then the waters had o-
verwhelmed us, the stream had
gone over our soul.

5 Then the proud waters
had gone over our soul.

6 Blessed be the Lord, who
hath not given us as a prey to
their teeth.

7 Our soul is escaped, as a
bird out of the snare of the
fowlers; the snare is broken,
and we are escaped.

8 Our help is in the name of
the lord, who made heaven
and earth.

PSALM CXXV.

THey that trust in the
Lord shall be as mount
Sion, which cannot be remov-
ed, but abideth for ever.

2 As the mountains are round
about Jerusalem, so the Lord is
round about his people, from
henceforth even for ever.

3 For the rod of the wicked
shall not rest upon the lot of
the righteous: lest the righteous put forth their hands unto
iniquity.

4 Do good, O Lord, unto those
that be good, and to them that
are upright in their hearts.

5 As for such as turn aside
unto their crooked ways, the
Lord shall lead them forth with

that dream.

2 Then wa
with laughter
with singing
among the h
hath done g
them.

3 The Lor
things for us,
glad.

4 Turn ag
O Lord, as t
south.

5 They that
reap in joy.

6 He that
weepeth, bea
shall doubtles
rejoicing, bri
with him.

PSAL

EXcept the
house.
vain that buil
Lord keep the
man waketh

2 It is vai
up early, to f
the bread of
he giveth his

3 Lo child
tage of the L
of the womb i

4 As arrow
of a mighty

PSALM CXXVIII.

1 Blessed is every one that feareth the Lord; that walketh in his ways.

2 For thou shalt eat the labour of thine hands: happy shalt thou be, and it shall be well with thee.

3 Thy wife shall be as a fruitful vine by the sides of thine house: thy children like olive-plants, round about thy table.

4 Behold, that thus shall the man be blessed that feareth the Lord.

5 The Lord shall bless thee out of Zion: and thou shalt see the good of Jerusalem, all the days of thy life.

6 Yea, thou shalt see thy children's children, and peace upon Israel.

PSALM CXXIX.

1 Many a time have they afflicted me from my youth, may Israel now say.

2 Many a time have they afflicted me from my youth: yet they have not prevailed against me.

3 The plowers plowed upon my back; they made long their furrows.

4 The Lord is righteous: he hath cut asunder the cords of the wicked.

5 Let them all be confounded, and turned back, that hate Zion.

6 Let them be as the grass upon the house-tops, which withereth afore it groweth up.

7 Wherewith the mower filleth not his hand, nor he that bindeth sheaves, his bosom.

8 Neither do they which go by, say, The blessing of the Lord be upon you: we bless you in the name of the Lord.

PSALM CXXX.

1 Out of the depths have I cried unto thee, O Lord.

2 Lord, hear my voice: let thine ears be attentive to the voice of my supplications.

3 If thou, Lord, shouldest mark iniquities, O Lord, who shall stand?

4 But there is forgiveness with thee, that thou mayest be feared.

5 I wait for the Lord, my soul doth wait, and in his word do I hope.

6 My soul waiteth for the Lord, more than they that watch for the morning: I say, more than they that watch for the morning.

7 Let Israel hope in the Lord: for with the Lord there is mercy: and with him is plenteous redemption.

8 And he shall redeem Israel from all his iniquities.

PSLAM CXXXI.

1 Lord, my heart is not haughty, nor mine eyes lofty: neither do I exercise myself in great matters, or in things too high for me.

2 Surely I have behaved and quieted myself as a child that is weaned of his mother; my

soul is even as a weaned child.

3 Let Israel hope in the Lord, from henceforth, and for ever.

PSALM CXXXII.

LORD, remember David, and all his afflictions.

2 How he sware unto the Lord, and vowed unto the mighty God of Jacob.

3 Surely I will not come into the tabernacle of my house, nor go up into my bed:

4 I will not give sleep to mine eyes, or slumber to mine eye lids,

5 Until I find out a place for the Lord: an habitation for the mighty God of Jacob.

6 Lo, we heard of it at Ephratah: we found it in the fields of the wood.

7 We will go into his tabernacles, we will worship at his footstool.

8 Arise, O Lord, into thy rest; thou, and the ark of thy strength.

9 Let thy priests be cloathed with righteousness, and let thy saints shout for joy.

10 For thy servant David's sake, turn not away the face of thine anointed.

11 The Lord hath sworn in

children also shall sit upon thy throne for ever more.

13 For the Lord hath chosen Zion: he hath desired it for his habitation.

14 This is my rest for ever: here will I dwell, for I have desired it.

15 I will abundantly bless her provision: I will satisfy her poor with bread.

16 I will also cloath her priests with salvation; and her saints shall shout aloud for joy.

17 There will I make the horn of David to bud: I have ordained a lamp for mine anointed.

18 His enemies will I clothe with shame, but upon himself shall his crown flourish.

PSALM CXXXIII.

BEhold how good and how pleasant it is for brethren to dwell together in unity.

2 It is like the precious ointment upon the head, that ran down upon the beard, even Aaron's beard, that went down to the skirts of his garments.

3 As the dew of Hermon, and as the dew that descended upon the mountains of Zion, so there the Lord commanded the blessing, even life for ever more.

PSALM CXXXIV.

3 The Lord that made heaven & earth, bless thee out of Zion.

PSALM CXXXV.

PRaise ye the Lord, praise ye the name of the Lord, praise him, O ye servants of the Lord.

2 Ye that stand in the house of the Lord, in the courts of the house of our God.

3 Praise ye the Lord, for the Lord is good: sing praises unto his name, for it is pleasant.

4 For the Lord hath chosen Jacob unto himself, and Israel for his peculiar treasure.

5 For I know that the Lord is great, and that our Lord is above all gods.

6 Whatsoever the Lord pleaseth, that did he in heaven, and in earth, in the seas, and all deep places.

7 He causeth the vapours to ascend from the ends of the earth, he maketh lightnings for the rain: he bringeth the wind out of his treasuries.

8 Who smote the first-born of Egypt, both of man and beast.

9 Who sent tokens and wonders into the midst of thee, O Egypt, upon Pharaoh, and upon all his servants.

10 Who smote great nations and slew mighty kings.

11 Sihon king of the Amorites, and Og king of Bashan, and all the kingdoms of Canaan:

12 And gave their land for an heritage, an heritage unto Israel his people.

13 Thy name, O Lord, endureth for ever, and thy memorial, O Lord, throughout all generations.

14 For the Lord will judge his people, and he will repent himself concerning his servants.

15 The idols of the heathen are silver and gold, the work of mens hands.

16 They have mouths, but they speak not: eyes have they, but they see not.

17 They have ears, but they hear not; neither is there any breath in their mouths.

18 They that make them are like unto them: so is every one that trusteth in them.

19 Bless the Lord, O house of Israel: bless the Lord, O house of Aaron.

20 Bless the Lord, O house of Levi; ye that fear the Lord, bless the Lord.

21 Blessed be the Lord out of Zion, which dwelleth at Jerusalem. Praise ye the Lord.

PSALM CXXXVI.

O Give thanks unto the Lord, for he is good: for his mercy endureth for ever.

2 O give thanks unto the God of gods: for his mercy endureth for ever.

3 O give thanks unto the Lord of Lords: for his mercy endureth for ever.

4 To him who alone doeth

great wonders : for his mercy endureth for ever.

5 To him that by wisdom made the heavens : for his mercy endureth for ever.

6 To him that stretched out the earth above the waters : for his mercy endureth for ever.

7 To him that made great lights : for his mercy endureth for ever.

8 The sun to rule by day : for his mercy endureth for ever.

9 The moon and stars to rule by night : for his mercy endureth for ever.

10 To him that smote Egypt in their first-born : for his mercy endureth for ever.

11 And brought out Israel from among them : for his mercy endureth for ever.

12 With a strong hand, and with a stretched out arm : for his mercy endureth for ever.

13 To him which divided the red sea into parts : for his mercy endureth for ever.

14 And made Israel to pass through the midst of it : for his mercy endureth for ever.

15 But overthrew Pharaoh and his host in the red sea : for his mercy endureth for ever.

16 To him which led his people through the wilderness : for his mercy endureth for ever.

17 To him which smote great kings : for his mercy endureth for ever.

18 And slew famous kings : for his mercy endureth for ever.

19 Shion king of the Amorites : for his mercy endureth for ever.

20 And Og the King of Bashan : for his mercy endureth for ever.

21 And gave their land for an heritage : for his mercy endureth for ever.

22 Even an heritage unto Israel his Servant : for his mercy endureth for ever.

23 Who remembered us in our low estate : for his mercy endureth for ever.

24 And hath redeemed us from our enemies : for his mercy endureth for ever.

25 Who giveth food to all flesh : for his mercy endureth for ever.

26 O give thanks unto the God of heaven : for his mercy endureth for ever.

PSALM CXXXVII.

BY the rivers of Babylon, there we sat down, yea, we wept when we remembred Zion.

2 We hanged our harps upon the willows, in the midst thereof.

3 For there they that carried us away captive, required of us a song ; and they that wasted us, required of us mirth, saying, Sing us one of the songs of Zion.

4 How shall we sing the Lord's song in a strange land ?

5 If I forget thee, O Jerusalem, let my right hand forget her cunning.

6 If I do not remember thee, let my tongue cleave to the roof of my mouth; if I prefer not Jerusalem above my chief joy.

7 Remember, O Lord, the children of Edom, in the day of Jerusalem; who said, Rase it, rase, even to the foundation thereof.

8 O daughter of Babylon, who art to be destroyed: happy shall he be that rewardeth thee, as thou has served us.

9 Happy shall he be that taketh and dasheth thy little ones against the stones.

PSALM CXXXVIII.

I Will praise thee with my whole heart, before the gods will I sing praise unto thee.

2 I will worship towards thy holy temple, and praise thy name for thy loving kindness, and for thy truth: for thou hast magnified thy word above all thy name.

3 In the day when I cried, thou answeredst me: and strengthenest me with strength in my soul.

4 All the kings of the earth shall praise thee, O Lord, when yet hath he respect unto the lowly: but the proud he knoweth afar off.

7 Though I walk in the midst of trouble, thou wilt revive me, thou shalt stretch forth thine hand against the wrath of mine enemies, and thy right hand shall save me.

8 The Lord will perfect that which concerneth me: thy mercy, O Lord, endureth for ever: forsake not the works of thine own hands.

PSALM CXXXIX.

O Lord, thou hast searched me, and known me.

2 Thou knowest my downsitting, and mine up-rising, thou understandest my thought afar off.

3 Thou compassest my path, and my lying down, and art acquainted with all my ways.

4 For there is not a word in my tongue, but lo, O Lord, thou knowest it altogether.

5 Thou hast beset me behind and before, and laid thine hand upon me.

6 Such knowledge is too wonderful for me; it is high, I cannot attain unto it.

7 Whither shall I go from thy spirit? or whither shall I

morning, and dwell in the uttermost parts of the sea:

10 Even there shall thy hand lead me, and thy right hand shall hold me.

11 If I say, surely the darkness shall cover me; even the night shall be light about me.

12 Yea, the darkness hideth not from thee, but the night shineth as the day: the darkness and the light are both alike to thee.

13 For thou hast possessed my reins: thou hast covered me in my mother's womb.

14 I will praise thee, for I am fearfully and wonderfully made: marvellous are thy works, and that my soul knoweth right well.

15 My substance was not hid from thee, when I was made in secret, and curiously wrought in the lowest parts of the earth

16 Thine eyes did see my substance, yet being unperfect, and in thy book all my members were written, which in continuance were fashioned: when as yet there was none of them.

17 How precious also are thy thoughts unto me, O God! how great is the sum of them!

me therefore ye bloody men.

20 For they speak against thee wickedly, and thine enemies take thy name in vain.

21 Do not I hate them, O Lord, that hate thee? and am not I grieved with those that rise up against thee?

22 I hate them with perfect hatred: I count them mine enemies.

23 Search me, O God, and know my heart: try me, and know my thoughts.

24 And see if there be any wicked way in me, and lead me in the way everlasting.

PSALM CXL.

DEliver me, O Lord, from the evil man: preserve me from the violent man.

2 Which imagine mischief in their heart: continually are they gathered together for war.

3 They have sharpened their tongues like a serpent; adders poison is under their lips. Selah.

4 Keep me, O Lord, from the hands of the wicked, preserve me from the violent man, who have purposed to overthrow my goings.

5 The proud have hid a snare for me, and cords: they have

7 O God the Lord, the strength of my salvation, thou hast covered my head in the day of battle.

8 Grant not O Lord, the desires of the wicked; further not his wicked device, lest they exalt themselves. Selah.

9 As for the head of those that compass me about, let the mischief of their own lips cover them.

10 Let burning coals fall upon them, let them be cast into the fire, into deep pits, that they rise not up again.

11 Let not an evil speaker be established in the earth: evil shall hunt the violent man to overthrow him.

12 I know that the Lord will maintain the cause of the afflicted, and the right of the poor.

13 Surely the righteous shall give thanks unto thy name: the upright shall dwell in thy presence.

PSALM CXLI.

LORD, I cry unto thee make haste unto me, give ear unto my voice when I cry unto thee.

2 Let my prayer be set forth before thee as incense, and the lifting up of my hands, as the evening sacrifice.

3 Set a watch, O Lord, before my mouth: keep the door of my lips.

4 Incline not my heart to any evil thing, to practice wicked works with men that work iniquity; and let me not eat of their dainties.

5 Let the righteous smite me, it shall be a kindness; and let him reprove me, it shall be an excellent oil, which shall not break my head: for yet my prayer also shall be in their calamities.

6 When their judges are overthrown in stony places, they shall hear my words, for they are sweet.

7 Our bones are scattered at the graves mouth, as when one cutteth and cleaveth wood upon the earth.

8 But mine eyes are unto thee, O God the Lord: in thee is my trust, leave not my soul destitute.

9 Keep me from the snare which they have laid for me, and the gins of the workers of iniquity.

10 Let the wicked fall into their own nets, whilst that I withal escape.

PSALM CXLII.

I Cried unto the Lord with my voice: with my voice unto the Lord did I make my supplication.

2 I poured out my complaint before him; I shewed before him my trouble.

3 When my spirit was overwhelmed within me, then thou knewest my path: in the way

wherein I walked, have they privily laid a snare for me.

4 I looked on my right hand, and beheld, but there was no man that would know me; refuge failed me: no man cared for my soul.

5 I cried unto thee, O Lord; I said, thou art my refuge and my portion, in the land of the living.

6 Attend unto my cry, for I am brought very low; deliver me from my persecutors, for they are stronger than I.

7 Bring my soul out of prison, that I may praise thy name: the righteous shall compass me about: for thou shalt deal bountifully with me.

PSALM CXLIII.

HEar my prayer, O Lord, give ear to my supplications: in thy faithfulness answer me, and in thy righteousness.

2 And enter not into judgement with thy servant: for in thy sight shall no man living be justified.

3 For the enemy hath persecuted my soul; he hath smitten my life down to the ground he hath made me to dwell in darkness, as those that have been long dead.

4 Therefore is my spirit overwhelmed within me; my heart within me is desolate.

5 I remember the days of old; I meditate on all thy works: I muse on the work of thy hands.

6 I stretch forth my hands unto thee: my soul thirsteth after thee, as the thirsty land. Selah.

7 Hear me speedily, O Lord, my spirit faileth: hide not thy face from me, lest I be like unto them that go down into the pit.

8 Cause me to hear thy loving kindness in the morning, for in thee do I trust: cause me to know the way wherein I should walk: for I lift up my soul unto thee.

9 Deliver me, O Lord, from mine enemies: I flee unto thee to hide me.

10 Teach me to do thy will, for thou art my God; thy spirit is good: lead me into the land of uprightness.

11 Quicken me, O Lord, for thy names sake; for thy righteousness sake bring my soul out of trouble.

12 And of thy mercy cut off mine enemies, and destroy all them that afflict my soul: for I am thy servant.

PSALM CXLIV.

BLessed be the Lord my strength, which teacheth my hands to war, and my fingers to fight.

2 My goodness, and my fortress, my high tower, and my deliverer, my shield, and he in whom I trust; who subdueth my people under me.

hat is man that
wledge of him?
nan, that thou
 of him?
e to vanity; his
1adow that paſſ-

eavens, O Lord,
vn; touch the
hey ſhall ſmoke.
 lightning, and
hoot out thine
tlroy them.
ē hand from a-
 and deliver me
 aters, from the
 children.
 outh ſpeaketh
 ir right hand is
 falſhood.
 new ſong unto
 upon a pſaltery
 nt of ten ſtrings
 es unto thee.
 hat giveth ſal-
 gs: who deli-
 s ſervant from
 d.
 and deliver me
 of ſtrange chil-
 outh ſpeaketh
 ir right hand is
 falſhood.
 ſons may be as
 in their youth;
 ers may be as
 oliſhed after the
 alace.
 arners may be
 all manner of
 ſheep may

bring forth thouſands, and ten thouſands in our ſtreets.

14 That our oxen may be ſtrong to labour; that there be no breaking in, nor going out; that there be no complaining in our ſtreets.

15 Happy is that people that is in ſuch a caſe: yea, happy is that people whoſe God is the Lord.

PSALM CXLV.

I Will extol thee, my God, O King: and I will bleſs thy name for ever and ever.

2 Every day will I bleſs thee. and I will praiſe thy name for ever and ever.

3 Great is the Lord, and greatly to be praiſed: and his greatneſs is unſearchable.

4 One generation ſhall praiſe thy works to another, and ſhall declare thy mighty acts.

5 I will ſpeak of the glorious honour of thy majeſty; and of thy wondrous works.

6 And men ſhall ſpeak o the might of thy terrible acts: & I will declare thy greatneſs.

7 They ſhall abundantly utter the memory of thy great goodneſs, and ſhall ſing of thy righteouſneſs.

8 The Lord is gracious and full of compaſſion: ſlow to anger, and of great mercy.

9 The Lord is good to all, and his tender mercies are over all his works.

10 All thy works ſhall praiſe

thee, O Lord: and thy saints shall bless thee.

11 They shall speak of the glory of thy kingdom, and talk of thy power.

12 To make known to the sons of men his mighty acts, and the glorious majesty of his kingdom.

13 Thy kingdom is an everlasting kingdom; and thy dominion endureth throughout all generations.

14 The Lord upholdeth all that fall: and raiseth up all those that be bowed down.

15 The eyes of all wait upon thee, and thou givest them their meat in due season.

16 Thou openest thine hand and satisfiest the desires of every living thing.

17 The Lord is righteous in all his ways, and holy in all his works.

18 The Lord is nigh unto all them that call upon him, to all that call upon him in truth.

19 He will fulfil the desire of them that fear him: he also will hear their cry, and will save them.

20 The Lord preserveth all them that love him: but all the wicked will he destroy.

21 My mouth shall speak the praise of the Lord; and let all flesh bless his holy name for ever and ever.

PSALM CXLVI.

Praise ye the Lord. Praise the Lord, O my soul.

2 While I live will I praise the Lord: I will sing praises unto my God, while I have any being.

3 Put not your trust in princes nor in the son of man, in whom there is no help.

4 His breath goeth forth, he returneth to his earth: in that very day his thoughts perish.

5 Happy is he that hath the god of Jacob for his help, whose hope is in the Lord his God.

6 Which made heaven and earth, the sea, and all that therein is: which keepeth truth for ever.

7 Which executeth judgment for the oppressed, which giveth food to the hungry: the lord looseth the prisoners.

8 The Lord openeth the eyes of the blind: the Lord raiseth them that are bowed down: the Lord loveth the righteous.

9 The Lord preserveth, the strangers: he relieveth the fatherless and widow, but the way of the wicked he turneth upside down.

10 The Lord shall reign for ever, even thy God, O Zion, unto all generations. Praise ye the Lord.

PSALM CXLVII.

Praise ye the Lord: for it is good to sing praises un-

to our God, for it is pleasant, and praise is comely.

2 The Lord doth build up Jerusalem, he gathereth together the out-casts of Israel.

3 He healeth the broken in heart, and bindeth up their wounds.

4 He telleth the number of the stars: he calleth them all by their names.

5 Great is our Lord, and of great power: his understanding is infinite.

6 The Lord lifteth up the meek: he casteth the wicked down to the ground.

7 Sing unto the Lord with thanksgiving: sing praise upon the harp unto our God.

8 Who covereth the heaven with clouds; who prepareth rain for the earth: who maketh grass to grow upon the mountains.

9 He giveth to the beast his food, and to the young ravens which cry.

10 He delighteth not in the strength of the horse: he taketh no pleasure in the legs of a man.

11 The Lord taketh pleasure in them that fear him, in those that hope in his mercy.

12 Praise the Lord, O Jerusalem, praise thy God, O Zion.

13 For he hath strengthened the bars of thy gates: he hath blessed thy children within thee

14 He maketh peace in thy borders, and filleth thee with the finest of the wheat.

15 He sendeth forth his Commandment upon earth: his word runneth very swiftly.

16 He giveth snow like wool: he scattereth the hoarfrost like ashes.

17 He casteth forth his ice like morsels: who can stand before his cold.

18 He sendeth out his word and melteth them: he causeth his wind to blow, and the waters flow.

19 He sheweth his word unto Jacob: his statutes and his judgments unto Israel.

20 He hath not dealt so with any nation: and as for his judgments they have not known them. Praise ye the Lord.

PSALM CXLVIII.

Praise ye the Lord. Praise ye the Lord from the heavens: praise him in the heights.

2 Praise ye him all his angels: praise ye him all his hosts.

3 Praise ye him sun and moon: praise him all ye stars of light.

4 Praise him ye heavens of heavens: and ye waters that be above the heavens.

5 Let them praise the name of the Lord, for he commanded, and they were created.

6 He hath also established them for ever and ever: he

hath made a decree which shall not pass.

7 Praise the Lord from the earth, ye dragons and all deeps.

8 Fire and hail, snow and vapour, stormy wind fulfilling his word.

9 Mountains and all hills: fruitful trees and all cedars.

10 Beasts and all cattle, creeping things and flying fowl.

11 Kings of the earth and all people: princes and all judges of the earth.

12 Both young men and maidens, old men and children.

13 Let them praise the name of the Lord, for his name alone is excellent; his glory is above the earth and heaven.

14 He also exalteth the horn of his people, the praise of all his saints; even of the children of Israel, a people near unto him. Praise ye the Lord.

PSALM CXLIX.

PRaise ye the Lord. Sing unto the Lord a new song, and his praise in the congregation of saints.

2 Let Israel rejoice in him that made him: let the children of Zion be joyful in their king.

3 Let them praise his name in the dance: let them sing praises unto him with the timbrel and harp.

4 For the Lord taketh pleasure in his people: he will beautify the meek with salvation.

5 Let the saints be joyful in glory: let them sing aloud upon their beds.

6 Let the high praises of God be in their mouth, and a two-edged sword in their hand;

7 To execute vengeance upon the heathen, and punishments upon the people;

8 To bind their kings with chains, and their nobles with fetters of iron.

9 To execute upon them the judgment written: this honour have all his saints. Praise ye the Lord.

PSALM CL.

PRaise ye the Lord. Praise God in his sanctuary: praise him in the firmament of his power.

2 Praise him for his mighty acts; praise him according to his excellent greatness.

3 Praise him with the sound of the trumpet: praise him with the psaltery and harp.

4 Praise him with the timbrel and dance: praise him with stringed instruments and organs.

5 Praise him upon the loud cymbals: praise him upon the high sounding cymbals.

6 Let every thing that hath breath praise the Lord. Praise ye the Lord.

The Proverbs of SOLOMON.

CHAP. I.

THE Proverbs of Solomon, the son of David, king of Israel.

2 To know wisdom and instruction, to perceive the words of understanding;

3 To receive the instruction of wisdom, justice, and judgment and equity.

4 To give subtilty to the simple, to the young man knowledge and discretion.

5 A wise man will hear, and will increase learning: and a man of understanding shall attain unto wise counsels.

6 To understand a proverb, and the interpretation; the words of the wise, and their dark sayings.

7 The fear of the Lord is the beginning of knowledge: but fools despise wisdom and instruction.

8 My son, hear the instruction of thy father, and forsake not the law of thy mother.

9 For they shall be an ornament of grace unto thy head, and chains about thy neck.

10 My son, if sinners entice thee consent thou not.

11 If they say, Come with us, let us lay wait for blood, let us lurk privily for the innocent without cause.

12 Let us swallow them up alive as the grave, & whole as those that go down into the pit.

13 We shall find all precious substance: we shall fill our houses with spoil.

14 Cast in thy lot among us, let us all have one purse.

15 My son, walk not thou in the way with them; refrain thy foot from their path.

16 For their feet run to evil, and make haste to shed blood.

17 Surely in vain the net is spread in the sight of any bird.

18 And they lay wait for their own blood: they lurk privily for their own lives.

19 So are the ways of every one that is greedy of gain, which taketh away the life of the owners thereof.

20 Wisdom crieth without, she uttereth her voice in the streets.

21 She crieth in the chief place of concourse, in the openings of the gates: in the city she uttereth her words, saying,

22 How long, ye simple ones will ye love simplicity? and the scorners delight in their scorning, and fools hate knowledge?

23 Turn you at my reproof: behold, I will pour out my spirit unto you, I will make known my words unto you.

24 Because I have called & ye refused; I have stretched out my hand, and no man regarded.

25 But ye have set at naught all my counsel, and would none of my reproof.

H

26 I also will laugh at your calamity, I will mock when your fear cometh:

27 When your fear cometh as desolation, and your destruction cometh as a whirlwind: when distress and anguish cometh upon you.

28 Then shall they call upon me, but I will not answer; they shall seek me early, but they shall not find me.

29 For that they hated knowledge, and did not chuse the fear of the Lord.

30 They would none of my counsel: they despised all my reproof.

31 Therefore shall they eat of the fruit of their own way, & be filled with their own devices.

32 For the turning away of the simple shall slay them, and the prosperity of fools shall destroy them.

33 But whoso hearkeneth unto me shall dwell safely, and shall be quiet from fear of evil.

CHAP. II.

MY son, if thou wilt receive my words, & hide my commandments with thee.

2 So that thou incline thine ear unto wisdom, and apply thine heart to understanding:

3 Yea, if thou criest after knowledge, and liftest up thy voice for understanding:

4 If thou seekest her as silver, and searchest for her as for hid treasures:

5 Then sha[ll]
stand the fear [of]
find the knowl[edge]

6 For the L[ord giveth wis]dom: out of h[is mouth cometh]
knowledge and [understanding]

7 He layet[h up sound wis]dom for the ri[ghteous: he is a]
buckler to the[m that walk up]rightly.

8 He keepe[th the paths of]
judgment, and [preserveth the]
way of his sain[ts]

9 Then sha[lt thou under]stand righteou[sness, and judg]ment, and equ[ity; yea, every]
good path.

10 When w[isdom entereth]
into thine hea[rt, and know]ledge is pleasa[nt unto thy soul]

11 Discretic[n shall preserve]
thee, understa[nding shall keep]
thee.

12 To deliv[er thee from the]
way of the evil [man, from the]
man that spe[aketh froward]
things.

13 Who lea[ve the paths of]
uprightness to [walk in the ways]
of darkness.

14 Who rej[oice to do evil,]
and delight in [the frowardness]
of the wicked.

15 Whose wa[ys are crooked,]
and they frowa[rd in their paths]

16 To deliv[er thee from the]
strange woman[, even from the]
stranger which [flattereth with]
her words.

17 Which for[saketh the guide]
of her youth, a[nd]

covenant of her God.

18 For her house inclineth unto death, and her paths unto the dead.

19 None that go unto her return again, neither take they hold of the paths of life.

20 That thou mayest walk in the way of good men, and keep the paths of the righteous.

21 For the upright shall dwell in the land, and the perfect shall remain in it.

22 But the wicked shall be cut off from the earth, and the transgressors shall be rooted out of it.

CHAP. III.

MY son, forget not my law, but let thine heart keep my commandments.

2 For length of days, and long life, and peace shall they add to thee.

3 Let not mercy and truth forsake thee: bind them about thy neck, write them upon the table of thine heart.

4 So shalt thou find favour and good understanding in the sight of God and man.

5 Trust in the lord with all thine heart, and lean not unto thine own understanding.

6 In all thy ways acknowledge him, and he shall direct thy paths.

7 Be not wise in thine own eyes: fear the Lord, and depart from evil.

8 It shall be health to thy navel, and marrow to thy bones.

9 Honour the Lord with thy substance, and with the first fruits of all thine increase.

10 So shall thy barns be filled with plenty, and thy presses shall burst out with new wine.

11 My son, despise not the chastning of the Lord, neither be weary of his correction.

12 For whom the Lord loveth he correcteth, even as a father the son in whom he delighteth.

13 Happy is the man that findeth wisdom, and the man that getteth understanding.

14 For the merchandise of it is better than the merchandise of silver; and the gain thereof than fine gold.

15 She is more precious than rubies, and all the things thou canst desire, are not to be compared unto her.

16 Length of days is in her right hand: and in her left hand riches and honour.

17 Her ways are ways of pleasantness, and all her paths are peace.

18 She is a tree of life to them that lay hold upon her: and happy is every one that retaineth her.

19 The Lord by wisdom hath founded the earth: by understanding hath he established the heavens.

20 By his knowledge the depths are broken up, and the clouds drop down the dew.

21 My son let not them depart from thine eyes: keep sound wisdom and discretion.

22 So shall they be life unto thy soul, and grace to thy neck,

23 Then shalt thou walk in thy way safely, and thy foot shall not stumble.

24 When thou liest down thou shalt not be afraid; yea, thou shalt lie down, and thy sleep shall be sweet.

25 Be not afraid of sudden fear, neither of the desolation of the wicked when it cometh.

26 For the Lord shall be thy confidence, and shall keep thy foot from being taken.

27 Withold not good from them to whom it is due, when it is in the power of thine hand to do it.

28 Say not unto thy neighbour, Go, and come again, and to-morrow I will give: when thou hast it by thee.

29 Devise not evil against thy neighbour, seeing he dwelleth securely by thee.

30 Strive not with a man without cause, if he have done thee no harm.

31 Envy thou not the oppressor, & chuse none of his ways.

32 For the froward is abomination to the Lord: but his secret is with the righteous.

33 The curse of the Lord is in the house of the wicked: but he blesseth the habitation of the just.

34 Surely he scorneth the scorners: but he giveth grace unto the lowly.

35 The wise shall inherit glory, but shame shall be the promotion of fools.

CHAP. IV.

Hear, ye children, the instruction of a father, and attend to know understanding.

2 For I give you good doctrine, forsake you not my law.

3 For I was my father's son, tender, and only beloved in the sight of my mother.

4 He taught me also, and said unto me, Let thy heart retain my words: keep my commandments and live.

5 Get wisdom, get understanding: forget it not, neither decline from the words of my mouth.

6 Forsake her not, and she shall preserve thee: love her, and she shall keep thee.

7 Wisdom is the principal thing: therefore get wisdom: and with all thy getting, get understanding.

8 Exalt her, and she shall promote thee: she shall bring thee to honour, when thou dost embrace her.

9 She shall give to thine head an ornament of grace: a crown of glory shall she deliver to thee.

10 Hear, O my son, and receive my sayings, and the

years of thy life shall be many.

11 I have taught thee in the way of wisdom: I have led thee in right paths.

12 When thou goest, thy steps shall not be straitned, and when thou runnest, thou shalt not stumble.

13 Take fast hold of instruction, let her not go; keep her, for she is thy life.

14 Enter not into the path of the wicked, and go not in the way of evil men.

15 Avoid it, pass not by it, turn from it, and pass away.

16 For they sleep not, except they have done mischief, and their sleep is taken away, unless they cause some to fall.

17 For they eat the bread of wickedness, and drink the wine of violence.

18 But the path of the just is as the shining light, that shineth more and more unto the perfect day.

19 The way of the wicked is as darkness: they know not at what they stumble.

20 My son, attend to my words: incline thine ear unto my sayings.

21 Let them not depart from thine eyes: keep them in the midst of thine heart.

22 For they are life unto those that find them, and health to all their flesh.

23 Keep thy heart with all diligence, for out of it are the issues of life.

24 Put away from thee a froward mouth, and perverse lips put far from thee.

25 Let thine eyes look right on, and let thine eye-lids look strait before thee.

26 Ponder the path of thy feet, and let all thy ways be established.

27 Turn not to the right hand, nor to the left, remove thy foot from evil.

CHAP. V.

MY son, attend unto my wisdom, and bow thine ear to my understanding.

2 That thou mayest regard discretion, and that thy lips may keep knowledge.

3 For the lips of a strange woman drop as an honey-comb, & her mouth is smoother than oil.

4 But her end is bitter as wormwood, sharp as a two-edged sword.

5 Her feet go down to death, her steps take hold on hell.

6 Lest thou shouldest ponder the path of life, her ways are moveable, that thou canst not know them.

7 Hear me now, therefore, O ye children, and depart not from the words of my mouth.

8 Remove thy way far from her, and come not nigh the door of her house.

9 Lest thou give thine honour unto others, and thy years

unto the cruel.

10 Lest strangers be filled with thy wealth, and thy labours be in the house of a stranger.

11 And thou mourn at the last, when thy flesh and thy body are consumed.

12 And say, How have I hated instruction, and my heart despised reproof?

13 And have not obeyed the voice of my teachers, nor inclined mine ear to them that instructed me.

14 I was almost in all evil, in the midst of the congregation and assembly.

15 Drink waters out of thine own cistern, and running waters out of thine own well.

16 Let thy fountains be dispersed abroad, and rivers of waters in the streets.

17 Let them be only thine own, & not strangers with thee.

18 Let thy fountain be blessed, and rejoice with the wife of thy youth.

19 Let her be as the loving hind, and pleasant roe; let her breasts satisfy thee at all times, and be thou ravished always with her love.

20 And why wilt thou, my

22 His own iniquities shall take the wicked himself, and he shall be holden with the cords of his sins.

23 He shall die without instruction, and in the greatness of his folly he shall go astray.

CHAP. VI.

MY son, if thou be surety for thy friend, if thou hast stricken thy hand with a stranger,

2 Thou art snared with the words of thy mouth, thou art taken with the words of thy mouth.

3 Do this now, my son, and deliver thyself, when thou art come into the hand of thy friend: go, humble thyself, and make sure thy friend.

4 Give not sleep to thine eyes, nor slumber to thine eyelids.

5 Deliver thyself as a roe from the hand of the hunter, and as a bird from the hand of the fowler.

6 Go to the ant, thou sluggard, consider her ways and be wise.

7 Which having no guide, overseer, or ruler,

8 Provideth her meat in the summer and gathereth her food in the harvest.

11 So shall thy poverty come as one that travaileth, and thy want as an armed man.

12 A naughty person, a wicked man, walketh with a froward mouth.

13 He winketh with his eyes, he speaketh with his feet, he teacheth with his fingers.

14 Frowardness is in his heart, he deviseth mischief continually, he soweth discord.

15 Therfore shall his calamity come suddenly: suddenly shall he be broken without remedy.

16 These six things doth the Lord hate, yea, seven are an abomination unto him.

17 A proud look, a lying tongue, and hands that shed innocent blood.

18 An heart that deviseth wicked imaginations: feet that be swift in running to mischief.

19 A false witness that speaketh lies, and him that soweth discord among brethren.

20 My son, keep thy father's commandment, and forsake not the law of thy mother.

21 Bind them continually upon thine heart, and tie them about thy neck.

22 When thou goest, it shall lead thee; when thou sleepest, it shall keep thee; and when thou awakest, it shall talk with thee.

23 For the commandment is a lamp, and the law is light; and reproofs of instruction are the way of life.

24 To keep thee from the evil woman, from the flattery of the tongue of a strange woman.

25 Lust not after her beauty in thine heart; neither let her take thee with her eye-lids.

26 For by means of a whorish woman, a man is brought to a piece of bread: and the adultress will hunt for the precious life.

27 Can a man take fire in his bosom, and his cloaths not be burnt?

28 Can one go upon hot coals, and his feet not be burnt?

29 So he that goeth into his neighbour's wife: whosoever toucheth her shall not be innocent.

30 Men do not despise a thief, if he steal to satisfy his soul, when he is hungry.

31 But if he be found, he shall restore seven fold, he shall give all the substance of his house.

32 But whoso committeth adultery with a woman, lacketh understanding: he that doth it, destroyeth his own soul.

33 A wound and dishonour shall he get, and his reproach shall not be wiped away.

34 For jealousy is the rage of a man, therefore he will not spare in the day of vengeance.

35 He will not regard any ransom: neither will he rest content, though thou givest many gifts.

CHAP. VII.

MY son, keep my words, and lay up my commandments with thee.

2 Keep my commandments, and live; and my law as the apple of thine eye.

3 Bind them upon thy fingers, write them upon the table of thine heart.

4 Say unto wisdom, Thou art my sister; and call understanding thy kinswoman.

5 That they may keep thee from the strange woman, from the stranger which flattereth with her words.

6 For at the window of my house I looked through my casement.

7 And beheld among the simple ones, I discerned among the youths, a young man void of understanding.

8 Passing through the street near her corner, and he went the way to her house.

9 In the twilight, in the evening, in the black and dark night.

10 And behold there met him a woman with the attire of an harlot, and subtil of heart.

11 (She is loud and stubborn, her feet abide not in her house.

12 Now is she without, now in the streets, and lieth in wait at every corner)

13 So she caught him and kissed him, and with an impudent face said unto him,

14 I have peace-offerings with me; this day have I payed my vows.

15 Therefore came I forth to meet thee, diligently to seek thy face, and I have found thee.

16 I have decked my bed with coverings of tapestry, with carved works, with fine linnen of Egypt.

17 I have perfumed my bed with myrrh, aloes and cinnamon.

18 Come, let us take our fill of love until the morning; let us solace ourselves with loves.

19 For the good man is not at home, he is gone a long journey.

20 He hath taken a bag of money with him, and will come home at the day appointed.

21 With her much fair speech she caused him to yield; with the flattering of her lips she forced him.

22 He goeth after her straitway, as an ox goeth to the slaughter, or as a fool to the correction of the stocks.

23 Till a dart strike through his liver, as a bird hasteth to the snare, and knoweth not that it is for his life.

24 Hearken unto me now, therefore, O ye children, and attend to the words of my mouth.

25 Let not thine heart decline to her ways; go not astray in her paths.

26 For she hath cast down many wounded; yea, many strong men have been slain by her.

27 Her house is the way to hell, going down to the chambers of death.

CHAP. VIII.

Doth not wisdom cry? and understanding put forth her voice?

2 She standeth in the top of high places, by the way, in the places of the paths.

3 She crieth at the gates, at the entry of the city, at the coming in of the doors.

4 Unto you, O men, I call & my voice is to the sons of man.

5 O ye simple, understand wisdom, and ye fools, be ye of an understanding heart.

6 Hear for I will speak of excellent things: and the opening of my lips shall be right things.

7 For my mouth shall speak truth, and wickedness is an abomination to my lips.

8 All the words of my mouth are in righteousness, there is nothing froward or perverse in them.

9 They are all plain to him that understandeth, and right to them that find knowledge.

10 Receive my instruction, and not silver; and knowledge rather than choice gold.

11 For Wisdom is better than rubies; and all the things that may be desired, are not to be compared to it.

12 I, wisdom, dwell with prudence, and find out knowledge of witty inventions.

13 The fear of the Lord is to hate evil: pride and arrogancy, and the evil way, and the froward mouth do I hate.

14 Counsel is mine, and sound wisdom: I am understanding, I have strength.

15 By me kings reign, and princes decree justice.

16 By me princes rule, and nobles, even all the judges of the earth.

17 I love them that love me, and those that seek me early shall find me.

18 Riches and honour are with me; yea, durable riches and righteousness.

19 My fruit is better than gold, yea, than fine gold; and my revenue than choice silver.

20 I lead in the way of righteousness, in the midst of the paths of judgment.

21 That I may cause those that love me to inherit substance: and I will fill their treasures.

22 The Lord possessed me in the beginning of his way, before his works of old.

23 I was set up from everlasting, from the beginning, or ever the earth was.

24 When there were no depths, I was brought forth;

when there were no fountains abounding with water.

25 Before the mountains were settled, before the hills was I brought forth.

26 While as yet he had not made the earth, nor the fields, nor the highest part of the dust of the world.

27 When he prepared the heavens, I was there: when he set a compass upon the face of the depth:

28 When he established the clouds above; when he strengthened the fountains of the deep.

29 When he gave to the sea his decree, that the waters should not pass his commandment; when he appointed the foundations of the earth:

30 Then I was by him, as one brought up with him; and I was daily his delight, rejoicing always before him:

31 Rejoicing in the habitable part of his earth, & my delights were with the sons of men.

32 Now, therefore, hearken unto me, O ye children: for blessed are they that keep my ways.

33 Hear instruction, and be wise, and refuse it not.

34 Blessed is the man that heareth me, watching daily at my gates, waiting at the posts of my doors.

35 For whoso findeth me, findeth life, and shall obtain favour of the Lord.

36 But he that sinneth against me, wrongeth his own soul: all they that hate me, love death.

CHAP. IX.

Wisdom hath builded her house, she hath hewn out her seven pillars.

2 She hath killed her beasts, she hath mingled her wine: she hath also furnished her table.

3 She hath sent forth her maidens, she crieth upon the highest places of the city.

4 Whoso is simple, let him turn in hither: as for him that wanteth understanding, she saith to him,

5 Come, eat of my bread, and drink of the wine which I have mingled.

6 Forsake the foolish, and live: and go in the way of understanding.

7 He that reproveth a scorner, getteth to himself shame: and he that rebuketh a wicked man, getteth himself a blot.

8 Reprove not a scorner, lest he hate thee: rebuke a wise man, and he will love thee.

9 Give instruction to a wise man, and he will be yet wiser: teach a just man, and he will increase in learning.

10 The fear of the Lord is the beginning of wisdom: and the knowledge of the holy is understanding.

11 For by me thy days shall

be multiplied: and the years of thy life shall be increased.

12 If thou be wise, thou shalt be wise for thyself: but if thou scornest, thou alone shalt bear it.

13 A foolish woman is clamorous; she is simple, and knoweth nothing.

14 For she setteth at the door of her house, on a seat in the high places of the city.

15 To call passengers, who go right on their ways.

16 Whoso is simple, let him turn in hither: and as for him that wanteth understanding, she saith to him,

17 Stolen waters are sweet, and bread eaten in secret is pleasant.

18 But he knoweth not that the dead are there, and that her guests are in the depths of hell.

CHAP. X.

THE Proverbs of Solomon. A wise son maketh a glad father: but a foolish son is the heaviness of his mother.

2 Treasures of wickedness profit nothing: but righteousness delivereth from death.

3 The Lord will not suffer the soul of the righteous to famish: but he casteth away the substance of the wicked.

4 He becometh poor that dealeth with a slack hand: but the hand of the diligent maketh rich.

5 He that gathereth in summer is a wise son: but he that sleepeth in harvest, is a son that causeth shame.

6 Blessings are upon the head of the just: but violence covereth the mouth of the wicked.

7 The memory of the just is blessed: but the name of the wicked shall rot.

8. The wise in heart will receive commandments: but a prating fool shall fall.

9 He that walketh uprightly, walketh surely: but he that perverteth his ways shall be known.

10 He that winketh with the eye causeth sorrow: but a prating fool shall fall.

11. The mouth of a righteous man is a well of life: but violence covereth the mouth of the wicked.

12 Hatred stirreth up strifes, but love covereth all sins.

13 In the lips of him that hath understanding, wisdom is found: but a rod is for the back of him that is void of understanding.

14 Wise men lay up knowledge: but the mouth of the foolish is near destruction.

15 The rich man's wealth is his strong city: the destruction of the poor is their poverty.

16 The labour of the righteous tendeth to life: the fruit of the wicked to sin.

17 He is in the way of life, that keepeth instruction: but he that refuseth reproof, erreth.

18 He that hideth hatred with lying lips, and he that uttereth a slander, is a fool.

19 In the multitude of words there wanteth not sin: but he that refraineth his lips is wise.

20 The tongue of the just is as choice silver: the heart of the wicked is little worth.

21 The lips of the righteous feed many: but fools die for want of wisdom.

22 The blessing of the Lord it maketh rich, and he addeth no sorrow with it.

23 It is as sport to a fool to do mischief: but a man of understanding hath wisdom.

24 The fear of the wicked it shall come upon him: but the desire of the righteous shall be granted.

25 As the whirlwind passeth, so is the wicked no more: but the righteous is an everlasting foundation.

26 As vinegar to the teeth, & as smoke to the eyes, so is the sluggard to them that send him.

27 The fear of the Lord prolongeth days: but the years of the wicked shall be shortned.

28 The hope of the righteous shall be gladness: but the expectation of the wicked shall perish.

29 The way of the Lord is strength to the upright: but destruction shall be to the workers of iniquity.

30 The righteous shall never be removed, but the wicked shall not inhabit the earth.

31 The mouth of the just bringeth forth wisdom: but the froward tongue shall be cut out

32 The lips of the righteous know what is acceptable but the mouth of the wicked speaketh frowardness.

CHAP. XI.

A False ballance is abomination to the Lord: bu a just weight is his delight.

2 When pride cometh, then cometh shame: but with the lowly is wisdom.

3 The integrity of the upright shall guide them: but the perverseness of transgressor shall destroy them.

4 Riches profit not in the day of wrath; but righteousness delivereth from death.

5 The righteousness of th perfect shall direct his way but the wicked shall fall by hi own wickedness.

6 The righteousness of th upright shall deliver them: bu transgressors shall be taken i their own naughtiness.

7 When a wicked man di eth, his expectation shall per ish: and the hope of unju men perisheth.

8 The righteous is deliver ed out of trouble: and th wic̶k̶e̶d̶ ̶c̶o̶m̶eth in his stead.

9 An hypocrite with his [mo]uth destroyeth his neigh[bo]ur: but through knowledge [a]ll the just be delivered.

10 When it goeth well with [th]e righteous, the city rejoic[et]h: and when the wicked [pe]rish there is shouting.

11 By the blessing of the [up]right, the city is exalted: [bu]t it is overthrown by the [m]outh of the wicked.

12 He that is void of wis[do]m, despiseth his neighbour: [bu]t a man of understanding [ho]ldeth his peace.

13 A tale-bearer revealeth [se]crets: but he that is of a [fa]ithful spirit concealeth the [m]atter.

14 Where no counsel is, the [pe]ople fall: but in the multitude [of] counsellors there is safety.

15 He that is surety for a [str]anger, shall smart for it: and [he] that hateth suretiship is sure.

16 A gracious woman re[ta]ineth honour: and strong [m]en retain riches.

17 The merciful man doth [go]od to his own soul: but he [th]at is cruel troubleth his own [fle]sh.

18 The wicked worketh a [de]ceitful work: but to him [th]at soweth righteousness, shall [be] a sure reward.

19 As righteousness tendeth [to] life; so he that pursueth evil, [pu]rsueth it to his own death.

20 They that are of a fro-

ward heart, are abomination to the Lord: but such as are upright in their way, are his delight.

21 Though hand join in hand the wicked shall not be unpunished: but the seed of the righteous shall be delivered.

22 As a jewel of gold in a swine's snout, so is a fair woman which is without discretion.

23 The desire of the righteous is only good: but the expectation of the wicked is wrath.

24 There is that scattereth and yet increaseth: and there is that withholdeth more than is meet: but it tendeth to poverty.

25 The liberal soul shall be made fat: and he that watereth shall be watered also himself.

26 He that withholdeth corn, the people shall curse him; but blessing shall be upon the head of him that selleth it.

27 He that diligently seeketh good, procureth favour: but he that seeketh mischief, it shall come unto him.

28 He that trusteth in his riches shall fall: but the righteous shall flourish as a branch.

29 He that troubleth his own house, shall inherit the wind: and the fool shall be servant to the wise of heart.

30 The fruit of the righteous is a tree of life: and he

that winneth souls is wise.

31 Behold the righteous shall be recompenced in the earth; much more the wicked and the sinner.

CHAP. XII.

WHoso loveth instruction, loveth knowledge: but he that hateth reproof is brutish.

2 A good man obtaineth favour of the Lord: but a man of wicked devices, will he condemn.

3 A man shall not be established by wickedness; but the root of the righteous shall not be moved.

4 A virtuous woman is a crown to her husband: but she that maketh ashamed, is as rottenness in his bones.

5 The thoughts of the righteous are right: but the counsels of the wicked are deceit.

6 The words of the wicked are to lie in wait for blood: but the mouth of the upright shall deliver them.

7 The wicked are overthrown and are not: but the house of the righteous shall stand.

8 A man shall be commended according to his wisdom: but he that is of a perverse heart, shall be despised.

9 He that is despised, and hath a servant, is better than he that honoureth himself, and lacketh bread.

10 A righteous man regardeth the life of his beast: but the tender mercies of the wicked are cruel.

11 He that tilleth his land shall be satisfied with bread: but he that followeth vain persons is void of understanding.

12 The wicked desireth the net of evil men: but the root of the righteous yieldeth fruit.

13 The wicked is snared by the transgression of his lips: but the just shall come out of trouble.

14 A man shall be satisfied with good by the fruit of his mouth: and the recompence of a man's hands shall be rendered unto him.

15 The way of a fool is right in his own eyes: but he that hearkeneth unto counsel is wise.

16 A fool's wrath is presently known: but a prudent man covereth shame.

17 He that speaketh truth sheweth forth righteousness: but a false witness, deceit.

18 There is that speaketh like the piercings of a sword: but the tongue of the wise is health.

19 The lip of truth shall be established for ever: but a lying tongue is but for a moment.

20 Deceit is in the heart of them that imagine evil: but to the counsellors of peace is joy.

21 There shall no evil happen to the just: but the wick-

d shall be filled with mischief.

22 Lying lips are abomination to the Lord: but they that deal truly, are his delight.

23 A prudent man concealeth knowledge: but the heart of fools proclaimeth foolishness.

24 The hand of the diligent shall bear-rule: but the slothful shall be under tribute.

25 Heaviness in the heart of man maketh it stoop: but a good word maketh it glad.

26 The righteous is more excellent than his neighbour: but the way of the wicked seduceth them.

27 The slothful man roasteth not that which he took in hunting; but the substance of a diligent man is precious.

28 In the way of righteousness is life, and in the pathway thereof there is no death.

CHAP. XIII.

A Wise son heareth his father's instruction: but a scorner heareth not rebuke.

2 A man shall eat good by the fruit of his mouth: but the soul of the transgressors shall eat violence.

3 He that keepeth his mouth keepeth his life: but he that openeth wide his lips, shall have destruction.

4 The soul of the sluggard desireth, and hath nothing: but the soul of the diligent shall be made fat.

5 A righteous man hateth lying: but a wicked man is loathsome, & cometh to shame.

6 Righteousness keepeth him that is upright in the way: but wickedness overthroweth the sinner.

7 There is that maketh himself rich, yet hath nothing: there is that maketh himself poor, yet hath great riches.

8 The ransom of a man's life are his riches: but the poor heareth not rebuke.

9 The light of the righteous rejoiceth: but the lamp of the wicked shall be put out.

10 Only by pride cometh contention: but with the well-advised is wisdom.

11 Wealth gotten by vanity shall be diminished: but he that gathereth by labour, shall increase.

12 Hope deferred maketh the heart sick: but when the desire cometh, it is a tree of life.

13 Whoso despiseth the word shall be destroyed: but he that feareth the commandment, shall be rewarded.

14 The law of the wise is a fountain of life; to depart from the snares of death.

15 Good understanding giveth favour: but the way of transgressors is hard.

16 Every prudent man dealeth with knowledge: but a fool layeth open his folly.

17 A wicked messenger falleth into mischief: but a faith-

ful ambassador is health.

18 Poverty and shame shall be to him that refuseth instruction: but he that regardeth reproof, shall be honoured.

19 The desire accomplished is sweet to the soul; but it is abomination to fools to depart from evil.

20 He that walketh with wise men shall be wise: but a companion of fools shall be destroyed.

21 Evil pursueth sinners: but to the righteous good shall be repayed.

22 A good man leaveth an inheritance to his children's children: and the wealth of the sinner is laid up for the just.

23 Much food is in the tillage of the poor: but there is that is destroyed for want of judgment.

24 He that spareth his rod, hateth his son: but he that loveth him chastneth him betimes.

25 The righteous eateth to the satisfying of his soul, but the belly of the wicked shall want.

CHAP. XIV.

Every wise woman buildeth her house: but the foolish plucketh it down with her hands.

2 He that walketh in his uprightness, feareth the Lord: but he that is perverse in his ways, despiseth him.

3 In the mouth of the foolish is a rod of pride: but the lips of the wise shall preserve them.

4 Where no oxen are, the crib is clean: but much increase is by the strength of the ox.

5 A faithful witness will not lie: but a false witness will utter lies.

6 A scorner seeketh wisdom, and findeth it not: but knowledge is easy unto him that understandeth.

7 Go from the presence of a foolish man when thou perceivest not in him the lips of knowledge.

8 The wisdom of the prudent is to understand his way: but the folly of fools is deceit.

9 Fools make a mock at sin: but among the righteous there is favour.

10 The heart knoweth his own bitterness: & a stranger doth not intermeddle with his joy.

11 The house of the wicked shall be overthrown: but the tabernacle of the upright shall flourish.

12 There is a way which seemeth right unto a man: but the end thereof are the ways of death.

13 Even in laughter the heart is sorrowful: and the end of that mirth is heaviness.

14 The backslider in heart shall be filled with his own ways: and a good man shall be satisfied from himself.

15 The simple believeth every word: but the prudent

29 He that is slow to wrath is of great understanding: but he that is hasty of spirit exalteth folly.

30 A sound heart is the life of the flesh, but envy the rottenness of the bones.

31 He that oppresseth the poor, reproacheth his maker: but, he that honoureth him, hath mercy on the poor.

32 The wicked is driven away in his wickedness: but the righteous hath hope in his death.

33 Wisdom resteth in the heart of him that hath understanding: but that which is in the midst of fools is made known.

34 Righteousness exalteth a nation: but sin is a reproach to any people.

35 The king's favour is toward a wise servant: but his wrath is against him that causeth shame.

CHAP. XV.

A Soft answer turneth away wrath: but grievous words stir up anger.

2 The tongue of the wise useth knowledge aright: but the mouth of fools poureth out foolishness.

3 The eyes of the Lord are in every place, beholding the evil and the good.

4 A wholesome tongue is a tree of life: but perverseness therein is a breach in the spirit.

5 A fool despiseth his father's instruction: but he that regardeth reproof is prudent.

6 In the house of the righteous is much treasure: but in the revenues of the wicked is trouble.

7 The lips of the wise disperse knowledge: but the heart of the foolish doth not so.

8 The sacrifice of the wicked is an abomination to the Lord: but the prayer of the upright is his delight.

9 The way of the wicked is an abomination unto the Lord, but he loveth him that followeth after righteousness.

10 Correction is grievous unto him that forsaketh the way: and he that hateth reproof shall die.

11 Hell and destruction are before the Lord; how much more then the hearts of the children of men?

12 A scorner loveth not one that reproveth him; neither will he go unto the wise.

13 A merry heart maketh a chearful countenance: but by sorrow of the heart the spirit is broken.

14 The heart of him that hath understanding seeketh knowledge; but the mouth of fools feedeth on foolishness.

15 All the days of the afflicted are evil; but he that is of a merry heart, hath a continual feast.

16 Better is little with the fear of the Lord, than great treasure, and trouble therewith.

17 Better is a dinner of herbs where love is, than a stalled ox, and hatred therewith.

18 A wrathful man stirreth up strife: but he that is slow to anger appeaseth strife.

19 The way of the slothful man is as an hedge of thorns; but the way of the righteous is made plain.

20 A wise son maketh a glad father; but a foolish man despiseth his mother.

21 Folly is joy to him that is destitute of wisdom; but a man of understanding walketh uprightly.

22 Without counsel purposes are disappointed; but in the multitude of counsellors they are established.

23 A man hath joy by the answer of his mouth; and a word spoken in due season how good is it.

24 The way of life is above to the wise, that he may depart from hell beneath.

25 The Lord will destroy the house of the proud; but he will establish the border of the widow.

26 The thoughts of the wicked are an abomination to the Lord: but the words of the

pure are pleasant words.

27 He that is greedy of gain troubleth his own house: but he that hateth gifts shall live.

28 The heart of the righteous studieth to answer; but the mouth of the wicked poureth out evil things.

29 The Lord is far from the wicked, but he heareth the prayer of the righteous.

30 The light of the eyes rejoiceth the heart: and a good report maketh the bones fat.

31 The ear that heareth the reproof of life, abideth among the wise.

32 He that refuseth instruction despiseth his own soul: but he that heareth reproof, getteth understanding.

33 The fear of the Lord is the instruction of wisdom; and before honour is humility.

CHAP. XVI.

THE preparations of the heart in man, and the answer of the Tongue is from the Lord.

2 All the ways of a man are clean in his own eyes, but the Lord weigheth the spirits.

3 Commit thy works unto the Lord and thy thoughts shall be established.

4 The Lord hath made all things for himself; yea even the wicked for the day of evil.

5 Every one that is proud in heart is an abomination to the Lord: though hand join in hand, he shall not be unpunished.

6 By mercy and truth iniquity is purged: and by the fear of the Lord men depart from evil.

7 When a man's ways please the Lord he maketh even his enemies to be at peace with him.

8 Better is a little with righteousness, than great revenues without right.

9 A man's heart deviseth his way: but the Lord directeth his steps.

10 A divine sentence is in the lips of the King: his mouth transgresseth not in judgment.

11 A just weight and ballance are the Lord's: all the weights of the bag are his work.

12 It is an abomination to kings to commit wickedness: for the throne is established by righteousness.

13 Righteous lips are the delight of kings: and they love him that speaketh right.

14 The wrath of a king is as messengers of death: but a wise man will pacify it.

15 In the light of the king's countenance is life: and his favour is as a cloud of the latter rain.

16 How much better is it to get wisdom than gold? and to get understanding, rather to be chosen than silver.

17 The High way of the upright is to depart from evil: he that keepeth his way, preserveth his soul.

18 Pride goeth before destruction; and an haughty spirit before a fall.

19 Better is it to be of an humble spirit with the lowly, than to divide the spoil with the proud.

20 He that handleth a matter wisely shall find good: and whoso trusteth in the Lord, happy is he.

21 The wise in heart shall be called prudent: and the sweetness of the lips increaseth learning.

22 Understanding is a wellspring of life unto him that hath it; but the instruction of fools is folly.

23 The heart of the wise teacheth his mouth, and addeth learning to his lips.

24 Pleasant words are as an honey-comb, sweet to the soul and health to the bones.

25 There is a way that seemeth right unto a man, but the end thereof are the ways of death.

26 He that laboureth, laboureth for himself, for his mouth craveth it of him.

27 An ungodly man digeth up evil, and in his lips there is a burning fire.

28 A froward man soweth strife; and a whisperer separateth chief friends.

29 A violent man enticeth his neighbour, and leadeth him into the way that is not good.

30 He shutteth his eyes to devise froward things, moving his lips he bringeth evil to pass.

31 The hoary head is a crown of glory, if it be found in the way of righteousness.

32 He that is slow to anger, is better than the mighty: and he that ruleth his spirit, than he that taketh a city.

33 The lot is cast into the lap, but the whole disposing thereof is of the Lord.

CHAP. XVII.

Better is a dry morsel, and quietness therewith than a house full of sacrifices with strife.

2 A wise servant shall have rule over a son that causeth shame, and shall have part of the inheritance among the brethren.

3 The fining pot is for silver and the furnace for gold: but the Lord trieth the hearts.

4 A wicked doer giveth heed to false lips, and a liar giveth ear to a naughty tongue.

5 Whoso mocketh the poor reproacheth his maker; and he that is glad at calamities, shall not be unpunished.

6 Childrens children are the crown of old men; and the glory of children are their fathers.

7 Excellent speech becometh not a fool; much less do lying lips a prince.

8 A gift is as a precious stone in the eyes of him that hath it; whithersoever it turneth it prospereth.

9 He that covereth a transgression seeketh love; but he that repeateth a matter separateth very freinds.

10 A reproof entereth more into a wise man, than an hundred stripes into a fool.

11 An evil man seeketh only rebellion, therefore a cruel messenger shall be sent against him.

12 Let a bear robbed of her whelps meet a man, rather than a fool in his folly.

13 Whoso rewardeth evil for good, evil shall not depart from his house.

14 The beginning of strife is as when one letteth out water; therefore leave off contention before it be meddled with.

15 He that justifieth the wicked, and he that condemneth the just, even they both are abomination to the Lord.

16 Wherefore is there a price in the hand of a fool to get wisdom, seeing he hath no heart to it.

17 A friend loveth at all times, and a brother is born for adversity.

18 A man void of understanding striketh hands, and becometh surety in the presence of his friend.

19 He loveth transgression that loveth strife; and he that exalteth his gate seeketh destruction.

20 He that hath a froward heart findeth no good; and he that a hath a perverse tongue, falleth into mischief.

21 He that begetteth a fool doth it to his sorrow; and the father of a fool hath no joy.

22 A merry heart doth good like a medicine; but a broken spirit drieth the bones.

23 A wicked man taketh a gift out of the bosom to pervert the ways of judgment.

24 Wisdom is before him that hath understanding; but the eyes of a fool are in the ends of the earth.

25 A foolish son is a grief to his father, and bitterness to her that bear him.

26 Also to punish the just is not good, nor to strike princes for equity.

27 He that hath knowledge spareth his words and a man of understanding is of an excellent spirit.

28 Even a fool, when he holdeth his peace, is counted wise; and he that shutteth his lips, is esteemed a man of understanding.   CHAP. XVIII.

THrough desire a man having separated himself,

The PROVERBS *of* SOLOMON.

seeketh and intermeddleth with all wisdom.

2 A fool hath no delight in understanding, but that his heart may discover it self.

3 When the wicked cometh, then cometh also contempt, and with ignominy reproach:

4 The words of a man's mouth are as deep waters, and the well-spring of wisdom as a flowing brook.

5 It is not good to accept the person of the wicked, to overthrow the righteous in judgment.

6 A fool's lips enter into contention, and his mouth calleth for strokes.

7 A fool's mouth is his destruction, and his lips are the snare of his soul.

8 The words of a tale-bearer are as wounds, and they go down into the innermost parts of the belly.

9 He also that is slothful in his work, is brother to him that is a great waster.

10 The name of the Lord is a strong tower, the righteous runneth into it, and is safe.

11 The rich man's wealth is his strong city; and as an high wall, in his own conceit.

12 Before destruction the heart of man is haughty, and before honour is humility.

13 He that answereth a matter before he heareth it, it is folly and shame unto him.

14 The spirit of a man will sustain his infirmity; but a wounded spirit who can bear?

15 The heart of the prudent getteth knowledge, and the ear of the wise seeketh knowledge.

16 A man's gift maketh room for him, and bringeth him before great men.

17 He that is first in his own cause seemeth just; but his neighbour cometh and searcheth him.

18 The lot causeth contentions to cease, and parteth between the mighty.

19 A brother offended is harder to be won than a strong city; and their contentions are like the bars of a castle.

20 A man's belly shall be satisfied with the fruit of his mouth, and with the increase of his lips shall he be filled.

21 Death and life are in the power of the tongue, and they that love it shall eat the fruit thereof.

22 Whoso findeth a wife findeth a good thing, and obtaineth favour of the Lord.

23 The poor useth intreaties, but the rich answereth roughly.

24 A man that hath friends must shew himself friendly; and there is a friend that sticketh closer than a brother.

CHAP. XIX.

BEtter is the poor that walketh in his integrity than

he that is perverse in his lips, and is a fool.

2 Also that the soul be without knowledge, it is not good; and he that hasteth with his feet sinneth.

3 The foolishness of a man perverteth his way, and his heart fretteth against the Lord.

4 Wealth maketh many friends; but the poor is separated from his neighbour.

5 A false witness shall not be unpunished; and he that speaketh lies shall not escape.

6. Many will intreat the favour of the prince: and every man is a friend to him that giveth gifts.

7 All the brethren of the poor do hate him: how much more do his friends go far from him he pursueth them with words, yet they are wanting to him.

8 He that getteth wisdom loveth his own soul: he that keepeth understanding shall find good.

9 A false witness shall not be unpunished: and he that speaketh lies shall perish.

10 Delight is not seemly for a fool: much less for a servant to have rule over princes.

11 The discretion of a man deferreth his anger, and it is his glory to pass over a transgression.

12 The king's wrath is as the roaring of a lion: but his favour is as dew upon the grass.

13 A foolish son is the calamity of his father, and the contentions of a wife are a continual dropping.

14 House and riches are the inheritance of fathers, and a prudent wife is from the Lord.

15 Slothfulness casteth into a deep sleep, and an idle soul shall suffer hunger.

16 He that keepeth the commandment, keepeth his own soul: but he that despiseth his ways shall die.

17 He that hath pity upon the poor, lendeth unto the Lord, and that which he hath given, will he pay him again.

18 Chasten thy son while there is hope: and let not thy soul spare for his crying.

19 A man of great wrath shall suffer punishment: for if thou deliver him, yet thou must do it again.

20 Hear counsel and receive instruction, that thou mayest be wise in thy latter end.

21 There are many devices in a man's heart: nevertheless, the counsel of the Lord, that shall stand.

22 The desire of a man is his kindness: and a poor man is better than a liar.

23 The fear of the Lord tendeth to life, and he that hath it, shall abide satisfied: he shall not be visited with evil.

24 A slothful man hideth

his hand in his bosom, and will not so much as bring it to his mouth again.

25 Smite a scorner and the simple will beware: and reprove one that hath understanding, and he will understand knowledge.

26 He that wasteth his father, and chaseth away his mother, is a son that causeth shame, and bringeth reproach.

27 Cease, my son, to hear the instruction that causeth to err from the words of knowledge.

28 An ungodly witness scorneth judgment: and the mouth of the wicked devoureth iniquity.

29 Judgments are prepared for scorners: and stripes for the back of fools.

CHAP. XX.

Wine is a mocker, strong drink is raging: and whosoever is deceived thereby is not wise.

2 The fear of a king is as the roaring of a lion: whoso provoketh him to anger, sinneth against his own soul.

3 It is an honour for a man to cease from strife: but every fool will be meddling.

4 The sluggard will not plough by reason of the cold; therefore shall he beg in harvest, and have nothing.

5 Counsel in the heart of man is like deep water: but a man of understa[nding]
it out.

6 Most men every one his but a faithful find?

7 The just his integrity; blessed after him

8 A king th throne of judg away all evil wi

9 Who can my heart clea from my sin.

10 Divers vers measures, alike abominati

11 Even a by his doing work be pure, be right.

12 The hear seeing eye, the even both of th

13 Love not come to pover eyes, and thou with bread.

14 It is naug saith the buyer, gone his way t

15 There i multitude of r lips of knowle ous jewel.

16 Take hi is surety for a take a pledge strange woman

17 Bread of

to a man, but afterwards his mouth shall be filled with gravel.

18 Every purpose is established by counsel; and with good advice make war.

19 He that goeth about as a tale-bearer, revealeth secrets; therefore meddle not with him that flattereth with his lips.

20 Whoso curseth his father or his mother, his lamp shall be put out in obscure darkness.

21 An inheritance may be gotten hastily at the beginning, but the end thereof shall not be blessed.

22 Say not thou, I will recompence evil; but wait on the Lord and he shall save thee.

23 Divers weights are an abomination unto the Lord; and a false ballance is not good.

24 Man's goings are of the Lord; how can a man then understand his own way?

25 It is a snare to the man who devoureth that which is holy; and after vows to make inquiry.

26 A wise king scattereth the wicked, and bringeth the wheel over them.

27 The spirit of man is the candle of the Lord, searching all the inward parts of the belly.

28 Mercy and truth preserve the king: and his throne is upholden by mercy.

29 The glory of young men is their strength: and the beauty of old men is the grey head.

30 The blueness of a wound cleanseth away evil: so do stripes the inward parts of the belly.

CHAP. XXI.

THE king's heart is in the hand of the Lord, as the rivers of water, he turneth it whithersoever he will.

2 Every way of a man is right in his own eyes: but the lord pondereth the hearts.

3 To do justice and judgment is more acceptable to the Lord than sacrifice.

4 An high look and a proud heart, and the plowing of the wicked is sin.

5 The thoughts of the diligent tend only to plentiousness; but of every one that is hasty, only to want.

6 The getting of treasures by a lying tongue, is a vanity tossed to and fro of them that seek death.

7 The robbery of the wicked shall destroy them, because they refuse to do judgment.

8 The way of man is froward and strange: but as for the pure his work is right.

9 It is better to dwell in a corner of the house-top, than with a brawling woman in a wide house.

10 The soul of the wicked desireth evil: his neighbour

findeth no favour in his eyes.

11 When the scorner is punished, the simple is made wise; and when the wise is instructed, he receiveth knowledge.

12 The righteous man wisely considereth the house of the wicked: but God overthroweth the wicked for their wickedness.

13 Whoso stoppeth his ears at the cry of the poor, he also shall cry himself, but shall not be heard.

14 A gift in secret pacifieth anger; and a reward in the bosom, strong wrath.

15 It is joy to the just to do judgment, but destruction shall be to the workers of iniquity.

16 The man that wandereth out of the way of understanding, shall remain in the congregation of the dead.

17 He that loveth pleasure shall be a poor man: he that loveth wine and oil shall not be rich.

18 The wicked shall be a ransom for the righteous, and the transgressor for the upright.

19 It is better to dwell in the wilderness than with a contentious and an angry woman.

20 There is a treasure to be desired, and oil in the dwelling of the wise: but a foolish man spendeth it up.

21 He that followeth after righteousness and mercy, findeth life, righteousness and honour.

22 A wise man scaleth the city of the mighty, and casteth down the strength of the confidence thereof.

23 Whoso keepeth his mouth and his tongue, keepeth his soul from troubles.

24 Proud and haughty scorner is his name, who dealeth in proud wrath.

25 The desire of the slothful killeth him; for his hands refuse to labour.

26 He coveteth greedily all the day long; but the righteous giveth and spareth not.

27 The sacrifice of the wicked is abomination: how much more when he bringeth it with a wicked mind.

28 A false witness shall perish: but the man that heareth speaketh constantly.

29 A wicked man hardneth his face: but as for the upright he directeth his way.

30 There is no wisdom nor understanding, nor counsel against the Lord.

31 The horse is prepared against the day of battle; but safety is of the Lord.

CHAP. XXII.

A Good name is rather to be chosen than great riches, and loving-favour rather than silver and gold.

2 The rich and poor meet together: the Lord is the m

...ter of them all.

3 A Prudent man foreseeth the evil, and hideth himself; but the simple pass on and are punished.

4 By humility and the fear of the Lord, are riches, and honour, and life.

5 Thorns and snares are in the way of the froward; he that doth keep his soul shall be far from them.

6 Train up a child in the way he should go; and when he is old he will not depart from it.

7 The rich ruleth over the poor, and the borrower is servant to the lender.

8 He that soweth iniquity shall reap vanity: and the rod of his anger shall fail.

9 He that hath a bountiful eye shall be blessed, for he giveth of his bread to the poor.

10 Cast out the scorner, and contention shall go out: yea, strife and reproach shall cease.

11 He that loveth pureness of heart, for the grace of his lips, the king shall be his friend.

12 The eyes of the Lord preserve knowledge, and he overthroweth the words of the transgressor.

13 The slothful man saith, There is a lion without, I shall be slain in the streets.

14 The mouth of strange women is a deep pit, he that is abhorred of the Lord shall fall therein.

15 Foolishness is bound in the heart of a child: but the rod of correction shall drive it far from him.

16 He that oppresseth the poor to increase his riches; and he that giveth to the rich, shall surely come to want.

17 Bow down thine ear, and hear the words of the wise, and apply thine heart unto my knowledge.

18 For it is a pleasant thing if thou keep them within thee; they shall withal be fitted in thy lips.

19 That thy trust may be in the Lord, I have made known to thee this day, even to thee.

20 Have not I written to thee excellent things in counsels and knowledge?

21 That I might make thee know the certainty of the words of truth: that thou mightest answer the words of truth to them that send unto thee.

22 Rob not the poor because he is poor; neither oppress the afflicted in the gate.

23 For the Lord will plead their cause, and spoil the soul of those that spoiled them.

24 Make no friendship with an angry man, and with a furious man thou shalt not go.

25 Lest thou learn his ways, and get a snare to thy soul.

26 Be not thou one of them that strike hands, or of them

that are sureties for debts.

27 If thou hast nothing to pay, why should he take away thy bed from under thee?

28 Remove not the ancient land-mark, which thy fathers have set.

29 Seest thou a man diligent in his business? he shall stand before kings, he shall not stand before mean men.

CHAP. XXIII.

WHen thou sittest to eat with a ruler, consider diligently what is before thee.

2 And put a knife to thy throat, if thou be a man given to appetite.

3 Be not desirous of his dainties, for they are deceitful meat.

4 Labour not to be rich; cease from thine own wisdom.

5 Wilt thou set thine eyes upon that which is not? for riches certainly make themselves wings, they fly away as an eagle towards heaven.

6 Eat thou not the bread of him that hath an evil eye, neither desire thou his dainty meats.

7 For as he thinketh in his heart, so is he: eat and drink saith he to thee, but his heart is not with thee.

8 The morsel which thou hast eaten shalt thou vomit up, and loose thy sweet words.

9 Speak not in the ears of a fool, for he will despise the wisdom of thy words.

10 Remove not the old land mark, and enter not into the fields of the fatherless.

11 For their redeemer is mighty: he shall plead their cause with thee.

12 Apply thine heart unto instruction, and thine ears to the words of knowledge.

13 Withold not correction from the child; for if thou beatest him with the rod, he shall not die.

14 Thou shalt beat him with the rod, and shalt deliver his soul from hell.

15 My son, if thine heart be wise, my heart shall rejoice even mine.

16 Yea, my reins shall rejoice, when thy lips speak right things.

17 Let not thine heart envy sinners, but be thou in the fear of the Lord all the day long.

18 For surely there is an end, and thine expectation shall not be cut off.

19 Hear thou my son, and be wise, and guide thine heart in the way.

20 Be not amongst wine bibbers, amongst riotous eaters of flesh.

21 For the drunkard and the glutton shall come to poverty, and drousiness shall cloth a man with rags.

22 Hearken unto thy father that begat thee, and despise not thy mother when she is old.

23 Buy the truth and sell it : also wisdom and instruction and understanding.

24 The father of the righteous shall greatly rejoice: and [he] that begetteth a wise child shall have joy of him.

25 Thy father and thy mother shall be glad, and she that bare thee shall rejoice.

26 My son, give me thine heart, and let thine eyes observe my ways.

27 For an whore is a deep ditch, and a strange woman is a narrow pit.

28 She also lieth in wait as for a prey, and increaseth the transgressors among men.

29 Who hath wo? who hath sorrow? who hath contentions? who hath babling? who hath wounds without cause? who hath redness of eyes?

30 They that tarry long at the wine, they that go to seek mixed wine.

31 Look not thou upon the wine when it is red, when it giveth his colour in the cup, when it moveth itself aright.

32 At the last it biteth like a serpent, and stingeth like an adder.

33 Thine eyes shall behold strange women, and thine heart shall utter perverse things.

34 Yea, thou shalt be as he that lieth down in the midst of the sea, or as he that lieth upon the top of a mast.

35 They have striken me, shalt thou say, and I was not sick; they have beaten me, and I felt it not: when shall I awake? I will seek it yet again.

CHAP. XXIV.

BE not thou envious against evil men, neither desire to be with them.

2 For their heart studieth destruction, and their lips talk of mischief.

3 Through wisdom is an house builded, and by understanding it is established.

4 And by knowledge shall the chambers be filled with all precious and pleasant riches.

5 A wise man is strong, yea, a man of knowledge increaseth strength.

6 For by wise counsel thou shalt make thy war: and in multitude of counsellors there is safety.

7 Wisdom is too high for a fool: he openeth not his mouth in the gate.

8 He that deviseth to do evil, shall be called a mischievous person.

9 The thought of foolishness is sin: and the scorner is an abomination to men.

10 If thou faint in the day of adversity, thy strength is small.

11 If thou forbear to deliver them that are drawn unto death, and those that are ready to be slain:

12 If thou sayest, Behold we knew it not: doth not he that pondereth the heart consider it? and he that keepeth thy soul, doth not he know it? and shall not he render to every man according to his works?

13 My son, eat thou honey because it is good, and the honey comb which is sweet to thy taste.

14 So shall the knowledge of wisdom be unto thy soul, when thou hast found it, then there shall be a reward, and thy expectation shall not be cut off.

15 Lay not weight, O wicked man, against the dwelling of the righteous: spoil not his resting place.

16 For a just man falleth seven times and riseth up again but the wicked shall fall into mischief.

17 Rejoice not when thine enemy falleth, and let not thine heart be glad when he stumbleth.

18 Lest the Lord see it, and it displease him, and he turn away his wrath from him.

19 Fret not thyself because of evil men, neither be thou envious at the wicked.

20 For there shall be no reward to the evil man, the candle of the wicked shall be put out.

21 My son, fear thou the Lord, and the king, and meddle not with them that are given to change.

22 For their calamity shall rise suddenly, and who knoweth the ruin of them both?

23 These things also belong to the wise. It is not good to have respect to persons in Judgment.

24 He that saith unto the wicked, Thou art righteous, him shall the people curse, nations shall abhor him.

25 But to them that rebuke him shall be delight, and a good blessing shall come upon them.

26 Every man shall kiss his lips that giveth a right answer.

27 Prepare thy work without, and make it fit for thyself in the field: and afterwards build thine house.

28 Be not a witness against thy neighbour without cause: and deceive not with thy lips.

29 Say not, I will do so to him as he hath done to me: I will render to the man according to his work.

30 I went by the field of the slothful, and by the vinyard of the man void of understanding.

31 And lo it was all grown over with thorns, and nettles had covered the face thereof, and the stone wall thereof was broken down.

32 Then I saw and considered it well, I looked upon it and received instruction.

33 Yet a little sleep, a little

umber, a little folding of the ands to sleep.

34. So shall thy poverty ome as one that travelleth, and ly want as an armed man.

CHAP. XXV.

These are also the Proverbs of Solomon, which the men of Hezekiah king of Judah copied out.

2 It is the glory of God to conceal a thing: but the honour of kings is to search out a matter.

3 The heaven for height, and the earth for depth, and the heart of kings is unsearchable.

4 Take away the dross from the silver, and there shall come forth a vessel for the finer.

5 Take away the wicked from before the king, and his throne shall be established in righteousness.

6 Put not forth thyself in the presence of the king, and stand not in the place of great men.

7 For better it is that it be said unto thee, Come up hither, than that thou shouldest be put lower in the presence of the prince whom thine eyes have seen.

8 Go not forth hastily to strive, lest thou know not what to do in the end thereof, when thy neighbour hath put thee to shame.

9 Debate thy cause with thy neighbour himself, and discover not a secret to another.

10 Lest he that heareth it put thee to shame, and thine infamy turn not away.

11 A word fitly spoken is like apples of gold, in pictures of silver.

12 As an ear-ring of gold and an ornament of fine gold, so is a wise reprover upon an obedient ear.

13 As the cold of snow in the time of harvest, so is a faithful messenger to them that send him: for he refresheth the soul of his masters.

14 Whoso boasteth himself of a false gift, is like clouds and wind without rain.

15 By long forbearing is a prince persuaded, and a soft tongue breaketh the bone.

16 Hast thou found honey? eat so much as is sufficient for thee: lest thou be filled therewith, and vomit it.

17 Withdraw thy foot from thy neighbour's house, lest he be weary of thee, & so hate thee.

18 A man that beareth false witness against his neighbour, is a maul, and a sword, and a sharp arrow.

19 Confidence in an unfaithful man in time of trouble, is like a broken tooth, and a foot out of joint.

20 As he that taketh away a garment in cold weather, and as vinegar upon nitre, so is he that singeth songs to an heavy

heart.

21 If thine enemy be hungry give him bread to eat: and if he be thirsty, give him water to drink.

22 For thou shalt heap coals of fire upon his head: and the Lord shall reward thee.

23 The north wind driveth away rain: so doth an angry countenance a back-biting tongue.

24 It is better to dwell in a corner of the house-top, than with a brawling woman and in a wide house.

25 As cold water to a thirsty soul, so is good news from a far country.

26 A righteous man falling down before the wicked, is as a troubled fountain and a corrupt spring.

27 It is not good to eat much honey: so for men to search their own glory, is not glory.

28 He that hath no rule over his own spirit, is like a city that is broken down, and without walls.

CHAP. XXVI.

AS snow in summer, and as rain in harvest, so honour is not seemly for a fool.

2 As the bird by wandering, as the swallow by flying, so the curse causeless shall not come.

3 A whip for the horse, a bridle for the ass, and a rod for the fool's back.

4 Answer not a fool according to his folly, lest thou also be like unto him.

5 Answer a fool according to his folly, lest he be wise in his own conceit.

6 He that sendeth a message by the hand of a fool, cutteth off the feet, & drinketh damage.

7 The legs of the lame are not equal: so is a parable in the mouth of fools.

8 As he that bindeth a stone in a sling, so is he that giveth honour to a fool.

9 As the thorn goeth up into the hand of a drunkard, so is a parable in the mouth of fools.

10 The great God that formed all things, both rewardeth the fool, and rewardeth the transgressor.

11 As a dog returneth to his vomit, so a fool returneth to his folly.

12 Seest thou a man wise in his own conceit? there is more hope of a fool than of him.

13 The slothful man saith There is a lion in the way: a lion is in the streets.

14 As the door turneth upon his hinges, so doth the slothful upon his bed.

15 The slothful hideth his hand in his bosom, it grieveth him to bring it again to his mouth.

16 The sluggard is wiser in his own conceit, than seven men that can render a reason.

17 He that passeth by and
meddleth with strife belonging
not to him, is like one that taketh a dog by the ears.
18 As a mad man who cast-
eth fire-brands, arrows and
death;
19 So is the man that decei-
veth his neighbour, and saith,
Am not I in sport?
20 Where no wood is, there
the fire goeth out; so where
there is no tale-bearer the strife
ceaseth.
21 As coals are to burning
coals, and wood to fire: so is
a contentious man to kindle
strife.
22 The words of a tale-
bearer are as wounds, and they
go down into the innermost
parts of the belly.
23 Burning lips and a wicked heart, are like a potsherd
covered with silver dross.
24 He that hateth dissemb-
leth with his lips, and layeth
up deceit within him.
25 When he speaketh fair
believe him not, for there are
seven abominations in his heart.
26 Whose hatred is covered
by deceit, his wickedness shall
be shewed before the whole
congregation.
27 Whoso diggeth a pit
shall fall therein: and he that
rolleth a stone, it will return
upon him.
28 A lying tongue hateth
those that are afflicted by it;
and a flattering mouth worketh
ruin.

CHAP. XXVII.

Boast not thyself of to-morrow; for thou knowest not
what a day may bring forth.

2 Let another man praise
thee and not thine own mouth;
a stranger, & not thine own lips.

3 A stone is heavy, and the
sand weighty; but a fool's
wrath is heavier than them
both.

4 Wrath is cruel, and anger
is outragious; but who is able
to stand before envy:

5 Open rebuke is better than
secret love.

6 Faithful are the wounds
of a friend, but the kisses of an
enemy are deceitful.

7 The full soul loatheth an
honey-comb; but to the hungry soul every bitter thing is
sweet.

8 As a bird that wandereth
from her nest, so is a man that
wandereth from his place.

9 Ointment and perfume rejoice the heart; so doth the
sweetness of a man's friend by
hearty counsel.

10 Thine own friend and
thy father's friend forsake not;
neither go into thy brother's
house in the day of thy calamity: for better is a neighbour
that is near, than a brother far
off.

11 My son, be wise and

make my heart glad, that I may answer him that reproacheth me.

12 A prudent man foreseeth the evil, and hideth himself: but the simple pass on and are punished.

13 Take his garment that is surety for a stranger, and take a pledge of him for a strange woman.

14 He that blesseth his friend with a loud voice, rising early in the morning, it shall be counted a curse to him.

15 A continual dropping in a very rainy day, and a contentious woman are alike.

16 Whosoever hideth her, hideth the wind, and the ointment of his right hand, which bewrayeth itself.

17 Iron sharpneth iron, so a man sharpneth the countenance of his friend.

18 Whoso keepeth the figtree, shall eat the fruit thereof: so he that waiteth on his master shall be honoured.

19 As in water face answereth to face: so the heart of man to man.

20 Hell and destruction are never full, so the eyes of man are never satisfied.

21 As the fining pot for silver, and the furnace for gold, so is a man to his praise.

22 Though thou shouldest bray a fool in a mortar among wheat with a pestle, yet will not his foolishness depart from him.

23 Be thou diligent to know the state of thy flocks, and look well to thy herds.

24 For riches are not for ever: and doth the crown endure to every generation?

25 The hay appeareth, and the tender grass sheweth itself, and herbs of the mountains are gathered.

26 The lambs are for thy cloathing, and the goats are the price of the field.

27 And thou shalt have goats milk enough for thy food, for the food of thy houshold, and for maintenance for thy maidens.

CHAP. XXVIII.

THE wicked flee when no man pursueth; but the righteous are bold as a lion.

2 For the transgression of a land, many are the princes thereof: but by a man of understanding and knowledge, the state thereof shall be prolonged.

3 A poor man that oppresseth the poor, is like a sweeping rain which leaveth no food.

4 They that forsake the law, praise the wicked: but such as keep the law contend with them

5 Evil men understand not judgment: but they that seek the Lord, understand all things.

6 Better is the poor that walketh in his uprightness, than he that is perverse in his ways

though he be rich.

7 Whoso keepeth the law is a wise son: but he that is a companion of riotous men, shameth his father.

8 He that by usury and unjust gain increaseth his substance, he shall gather it for him that will pity the poor.

9 He that turneth away his ear from hearing the law, even his prayer shall be abomination.

10 Whoso causeth the righteous to go astray in an evil way, he shall fall himself into his own pit: but the upright shall have good things in possession.

11 The rich man is wise in his own conceit: but the poor that hath understanding searcheth him out.

12 When righteous men do rejoice, there is great glory, but when the wicked rise, a man is hidden.

13 He that covereth his sins shall not prosper: but whoso confesseth and forsaketh them, shall have mercy.

14 Happy is the man that feareth alway: but he that hardneth his heart shall fall into mischief.

15 As a roaring lion, and a ranging bear, so is a wicked ruler over the poor people.

16 The prince that wanteth understanding, is also a great oppressor: but he that hateth covetousness shall prolong his days.

17 A man that doth violence to the blood of any person, shall flee to the pit, let no man stay him.

18 Whoso walketh uprightly shall be saved: but he that is perverse in his ways shall fall at once.

19 He that tilleth his land shall have plenty of bread: but he that followeth after vain persons, shall have poverty enough.

20 A faithful man shall abound with blessings; but he that maketh haste to be rich, shall not be innocent.

21 To have respect of persons is not good: for a piece of bread that man will transgress.

22 He that hasteth to be rich hath an evil eye, and considereth not that poverty shall come upon him.

23 He that rebuketh a man, afterwards shall find more favour than he that flattereth with the tongue.

24 Whoso robbeth his father or his mother, and saith It is no transgression, the same is the companion of a destroyer.

25 He that is of a proud heart, stirreth up strife: but he that putteth his trust in the Lord shall be made fat.

26 He that trusteth in his own heart is a fool: but whoso walketh wisely, he shall be

delivered.

27 He that giveth unto the poor, shall not lack: but he that hideth his eyes shall have many a curse.

28 When the wicked rise, men hide themselves: but when they perish, the righteous increase.

CHAP. XXIX.

HE that being often reproved, hardneth his neck, shall suddenly be destroyed, and that without remedy.

2 When the righteous are in authority, the people rejoice: but when the wicked beareth rule, the people mourn.

3 Whoso loveth wisdom rejoiceth his father: but he that keepeth company with harlots, spendeth his substance.

4 The king by judgment establisheth the land: but he that receiveth gifts, overthroweth it.

5 A man that flattereth his neighbour, spreadeth a net for his feet.

6 In the transgression of an evil man there is a snare: but the righteous doth sing and rejoice.

7 The righteous considereth the cause of the poor: but the wicked regardeth not to know it.

8 Scornful men bring a city into a snare: but wise men turn away wrath.

9 If a wise man contendeth with a foolish man, whether he rage or laugh, there is no rest.

10 The blood-thirsty hate the upright: but the just seek his soul.

11 A fool uttereth all his mind, but a wise man keepeth it in till afterwards.

12 If a ruler hearken to lies, all his servants are wicked.

13 The poor and the deceitful man meet together: the Lord lightneth both their eyes.

14 The king that faithfully judgeth the poor, his throne shall be established for ever.

15 The rod and reproof give wisdom: but a child left to himself, bringeth his mother to shame.

16 When the wicked are multiplied, transgression increaseth: but the righteous shall see their fall.

17 Correct thy son, and he shall give thee rest: yea, he shall give delight unto thy soul.

18 Where there is no vision the people perish: but he that keepeth the law, happy is he.

19 A servant will not be corrected by words: for though he understand, he will not answer.

20 Seest thou a man that is hasty in his words? there is more hope of a fool than of him.

21 He that delicately bringeth up his servant from a child, shall have him become his son at the length.

22 An angry man stirreth up strife, and a furious man aboundeth in transgression.

23 A man's pride shall bring him low: but honour shall uphold the humble in spirit.

24 Whoso is partner with a thief, hateth his own soul: he heareth cursing, and bewrayeth it not.

25 The fear of man bringeth a snare; but whoso putteth his trust in the Lord, shall be safe.

26 Many seek the ruler's favour, but every man's judgment cometh from the Lord.

27 An unjust man is an abomination to the just: and he that is upright in the way, is abomination to the wicked.

CHAP. XXX.

THE words of Agur the son of Jakeh, even the prophecy: the man spake unto Ithiel, even unto Ithiel and Ucal.

2 Surely I am more brutish than any man, and have not the understanding of a man.

3 I neither learned wisdom, nor have the knowledge of the holy.

4 Who hath ascended up into heaven, or descended? who hath gathered the wind in his fists? who hath bound the waters in a garment? who hath established all the ends of the earth? what is his name, and what is his son's name, if thou canst tell?

5 Every word of God is pure: he is a shield unto them that put their trust in him.

6 Add thou not unto his words, lest he reprove thee, and thou be found a liar.

7 Two things have I required of thee, deny me them not before I die.

8 Remove far from me vanity and lies: give me neither poverty nor riches, feed me with food convenient for me.

9 Lest I be full and deny thee, and say, who is the Lord? or lest I be poor and steal, and take the name of my God in vain.

10 Accuse not a servant unto his master, lest he curse thee, and thou be found guilty.

11 There is a generation that curseth their father, and doth not bless their mother.

12 There is a generation that are pure in their own eyes, and yet is not washed from their filthiness.

13 There is a generation, O how lofty are their eyes? and their eye lids are lifted up.

14 There is a generation whose teeth are as swords, and their jaw-teeth as knives, to devour the poor from off the earth, and the needy from among men.

15 The horse-leach hath two daughters, crying Give, give. There are three things

that are never satisfied, yea four things say not, It is enough.

16 The grave, and the barren womb, the earth that is not filled with water, and the fire that saith not, It is enough.

17 The eye that mocketh at his father, and despiseth to obey his mother, the ravens of the valley shall pick it out, and the young eagles shall eat it.

18 There be three things which are too wonderful for me, yea, four which I know not.

19 The way of an eagle in the air, the way of a serpent upon a rock, the way of a ship in the midst of the sea, and the way of a man with a maid.

20 Such is the way of an adulterous woman: she eateth and wipeth her mouth, and saith I have done no wickedness.

21 For three things the earth is disquieted, and for four which it cannot bear.

22 For a servant when he reigneth, and a fool when he is filled with meat.

23 For an odious woman when she is married, and an handmaid that is heir to her mistress.

24 There be four things which are little upon the earth, but they are exceeding wise.

25 The ants are a people not strong, yet they prepare their meat in the summer.

26 The conies are but a feeble folk, yet make they their houses in the rocks.

27 The locusts have no king, yet go they forth all of them by bands.

28 The spider taketh hold with her hands, and is in kings palaces.

29 There be three things which go well, yea, four are comely in going.

30 A lion which is strongest among beasts, and turneth not away for any.

31 A grey-hound and he-goat also, and a king, against whom there is no rising up.

32 If thou hast done foolishly in lifting up thyself, or if thou hast thought evil, lay thine hand upon thy mouth.

33 Surely the churning of milk bringeth forth butter, and the wringing of the nose bringeth forth blood: so the forcing of wrath bringeth forth strife.

CHAP. XXXI.

THE words of King Lemuel, the prophecy that his mother taught him.

2 What, my son! and what the son of my womb! and what the son of my vows!

3 Give not thy strength unto women, nor thy ways to that which destroyeth kings.

4 It is not for kings, O Lemuel, it is not for kings to drink wine, nor for princes strong drink.

5 Lest they drink and forget the law, and pervert the judg

The PROVERBS *of* SOLOMON.   151

ment of any of the afflicted.

6 Give strong drink unto him that is ready to perish, and wine to those that be of heavy hearts.

7 Let him drink and forget his poverty, and remember his misery no more.

8 Open thy mouth for the dumb in the cause of all such as are appointed to destruction.

9 Open thy mouth, judge righteously, and plead the cause of the poor and needy.

10 Who can find a virtuous woman? for her price is far above rubies.

11 The heart of her husband doth safely trust in her, so that he shall have no need of spoil.

12 She will do him good and not evil, all the days of her life.

13 She seeketh wool, and flax, and worketh willingly with her hands.

14 She is like the merchants ships, she bringeth her food from afar.

15 She riseth also while it is yet night, and giveth meat to her houshold, and a portion to her maidens.

16 She considereth a field, and buyeth it: with the fruit of her hands she planteth a vinyard.

17 She girdeth her loins with strength, and strengtheneth her arms.

18 She perceiveth that her merchandize is good: her candle goeth not out by night.

19 She layeth her hands to the spindle, and her hands hold the distaff.

20 She stretcheth out her hand to the poor; yea, she reacheth forth her hands to the needy.

21 She is not afraid of the snow for her houshold: for all her houshold are clothed with scarlet.

22 She maketh herself coverings of tapestry, her cloathing is silk and purple.

23 Her husband is known in the gates, when he sitteth among the elders of the land.

24 She maketh fine linnen and selleth it, and delivereth girdles unto the merchant.

25 Strength and honour are her cloathing; and she shall rejoice in time to come.

26 She openeth her mouth with wisdom, and in her tongue is the law of kindness.

27 She looketh well to the ways of her houshold, and eateth not the bread of idleness.

28 Her children arise up and call her blessed; her husband also, and he praiseth her.

29 Many daughters have done vertuously, but thou excellest them all.

30 Favour is deceitful and beauty is vain; but a woman that feareth the Lord, she shall be praised.

31 Give her of the fruit of her hands, and let her own works praise her in the gates.

The END *of the* PROVERBS.

CHRIST's SERMON on the Mount, contained in the V. VI. and VII. Chapters of St. Matthew's Gospel.

CHAP. V.

AND seeing the multitudes, he went up into a mountain; and when he was set, his disciples came unto him.

2 And he opened his mouth and taught them, saying,

3 Blessed are the poor in spirit, for theirs is the kingdom of heaven.

4 Blessed are they that mourn: for they shall be comforted.

5 Blessed are the meek: for they shall inherit the earth.

6 Blessed are they which do hunger and thirst after righteousness: for they shall be filled.

7 Blessed are the merciful: for they shall obtain mercy.

8 Blessed are the pure in heart: for they shall see God.

9 Blessed are the peace-makers for they shall be called the children of God.

10 Blessed are they which are persecuted for righteousness sake: for theirs is the kingdom of heaven.

11 Blessed are ye when men shall revile you, and persecute you, and shall say all manner of evil against you falsely for my sake.

12 Rejoice and be exceeding glad, for great is your reward in heaven: for so persecuted they the prophets which were before you.

13 Ye are the salt of the earth: but if the salt have lost his savour, wherewith shall it be salted? it is thenceforth good for nothing but to be cast out, and to be trodden under foot of men.

14 Ye are the light of the world: a city that is set on an hill cannot be hid.

15 Neither do men light a candle and put it under a bushel, but on a candlestick, and it giveth light unto all that are in the house.

16 Let your light so shine before men, that they may see your good works, and glorify your father which is in heaven.

17 Think not that I am come to destroy the law or the prophets: I am not come to destroy, but to fulfil.

18 For verily I say unto you, till heaven and earth pass, one jot or one title shall in no wise pass from the law, till all be fulfilled.

19 Whosoever therefore shall break one of these least commandments, & shall teach men so, he shall be called the least in the kingdom of heaven: but whosoever shall do and teach them, the same shall be called great in the kingdom of heaven.

20 For I say unto you, that except your righteousness shall exceed the righteousness of the

scribes and pharisees, ye shall in no case enter into the kingdom of heaven.

21 Ye have heard that it was said by them of old time, Thou shalt not kill: and whosoever shall kill shall be in danger of the judgment.

22 But I say unto you, that whosoever is angry with his brother without a cause, shall be in danger of the judgment: and whosoever shall say to his brother, Raca, shall be in danger of the counsel: but whosoever shall say, Thou fool, shall be in danger of hell-fire.

23 Therefore if thou bring thy gift to the altar, and there remembrest that thy brother hath aught against thee.

24 Leave there thy gift before the altar, and go thy way, first be reconciled to thy brother, and then come and offer thy gift.

25 Agree with thine adversary quickly, whiles thou art in the way with him: lest at any time the adversary deliver thee to the judge, and the judge deliver thee to the officer and thou be cast into prison.

26 Verily I say unto thee, thou shalt by no means come out thence till thou hast paid the uttermost farthing.

27 Ye have heard that it was said by them of old time, Thou shalt not commit adultery.

28 But I say unto you, that whosoever looketh on a woman to lust after her, hath commited adultery with her already in his heart.

29 And if thy right eye offend thee, pluck it out and cast it from thee; for it is profitable for thee that one of thy members should perish, and not that thy whole body should be cast into hell.

30 And if thy right hand offend thee, cut it off, and cast it from thee; for it is profitable for thee that one of thy members should perish, and not that thy whole body should be cast into hell.

31 It hath been said, Whosoever shall put away his wife, let him give her a writing of divorcement.

32 But I say unto you, that whosoever shall put away his wife, saving for the cause of fornication, causeth her to commit adultery; and whosoever shall marry her that is divorced, committeth adultery.

33 Again ye have heard that it hath been said by them of old time, Thou shalt not forswear thyself, but shalt perform unto the Lord thine oaths.

34 But I say unto you, Swear not at all, neither by heaven, for it is God's throne;

35 Nor by the earth, for it is his foot-stool: nether by Jerusalem, for it is the city of

the great king.

36 Neither shalt thou swear by thy head, because thou canst not make one hair white or black.

37 But let your communication be Yea, yea; Nay, nay, for whatsoever is more than these, cometh of evil.

38 Ye have heard that it hath been said, An eye for an eye, and a tooth for a tooth.

39 But I say unto you that ye resist not evil: but whosoever shall smite thee on thy right cheek, turn to him the other also.

40 And if any man will sue thee at the law, and take away thy coat, let him have thy cloak also.

41 And whosoever shall compel thee to go a mile, go with him twain.

42 Give to him that asketh thee; and from him that would borrow of thee turn not thou away.

43 Ye have heard that it hath been said, Thou shalt love thy neighbour and hate thine enemy.

44 But I say unto you, Love your enemies, bless them that curse you, do good to them that hate you, and pray for them which despitefully use you, and persecute you.

45 That ye may be the children of your father which is in heaven: for he maketh his sun to rise on the evil and on the good, and sendeth rain on the just and on the unjust.

46 For if ye love them which love you, what reward have ye? Do not even the publicans the same?

47 And if ye salute your brethren only, what do ye more than others? Do not even the publicans so?

48 Be ye therefore perfect, even as your father which is in heaven is perfect.

CHAP. VI.

TAke heed that ye do not your alms before men, to be seen of them: otherwise you have no reward of your father which is in heaven.

2 Therefore, when thou dost thine alms, do not sound a trumpet before thee, as the hypocrites do, in the synagogues, and in the streets, that they may have glory of men. Verily, I say unto you, they have their reward.

3 But when thou dost alms, let not thy left hand know what thy right hand doeth:

4 That thine alms may be in secret: and thy father which seeth in secret, himself shall reward thee openly.

5 And when thou prayest, thou shalt not be as the hypocrites are: for they love to pray standing in the synagogues and in the corners of the streets, that they may be

seen of men. Verily I say unto you they have their reward.

6 But thou when thou prayest, enter into thy closet, and when thou hast shut thy door, pray to thy father which is in secret, and thy father which seeth in secret, shall reward thee openly.

7 But when ye pray, use not vain repetitions, as the heathen do; for they think that they shall be heard for their much speaking.

8 Be not ye therefore like unto them: for your father knoweth what things ye have need of, before ye ask him.

9 After this manner therefore pray ye: Our father which art in heaven, hallowed be thy name.

10 Thy kingdom come. Thy will be done in earth as it is in heaven.

11 Give us this day our daily bread.

12 And forgive us our debts, as we forgive our debtors:

13 And lead us not into temptation, but deliver us from evil: for thine is the kingdom, and the power, and the glory, for ever. Amen.

14 For if ye forgive men their trespasses, your heavenly father will also forgive you.

15 But if ye forgive not men their trespasses, neither will your father forgive your trespasses.

16 Moreover, when ye fast, be not as the hypocrites, of a sad countenance: for they disfigure their faces, that they may appear unto men to fast. Verily I say unto you they have their reward.

17 But thou when thou fastest, anoint thine head, and wash thy face.

18 That thou appear not unto men to fast, but unto thy father which is in secret, and thy father which seeth in secret shall reward thee openly.

19 Lay not up for yourselves treasures upon earth, where moth and rust doth corrupt, and where thieves break thro' and steal.

20 But lay up for yourselves treasures in heaven, where neither moth nor rust doth corrupt, and where thieves do not break through nor steal.

21 For where your treasure is, there will your heart be also.

22 The light of the Body is the eye: if therefore thine eye be single, thy whole body shall be full of light.

23 But if thine eye be evil, thy whole body shall be full of darkness. If therefore the light that is in thee be darkness, how great is that darkness?

24 No man can serve two masters: for either he will hate the one, and love the other; or else he will hold to the one, and despise the other. Ye can-

not serve God and mammon.

25 Therefore I say unto you, Take no thought for your life, what ye shall eat, or what ye shall drink; nor yet for your body, what ye shall put on: Is not the life more than meat, and the body than raiment?

26 Behold the fowls of the air; for they sow not, neither do they reap, nor gather into barns; yet your heavenly father feedeth them. Are not ye much better than they?

27 Which of you by taking thought can add one cubit unto his stature?

28 And why take ye tho't for raiment? Consider the lillies of the field how they grow: they toil not, neither do they spin.

29 And yet I say unto you, that even Solomon, in all his glory, was not array'd like one of these.

30 Wherefore if God so clothe the grass of the field, which to-day is, and to-morrow is cast into the oven: shall he not much more clothe you, O ye of little faith?

31 Therefore take no tho't saying, What shall we eat? or what shall we drink? or wherewithal shall we be clothed?

32 (For after all these things do the gentiles seek) for your heavenly father knoweth that ye have need of all these things.

33 But seek ye first the king-dom of God, and his righteousness, and all these things shall be added unto you.

34 Take therefore no tho't for the morrow: for the morrow shall take thought for the things of itself: sufficient unto the day is the evil thereof.

CHAP. VII.

JUdge not, that ye be not judged.

2 For with what judgment ye judge, ye shall be judged; and with what measure ye mete, it shall be measured to you again.

3 And why beholdest thou the mote that is in thy brother's eye, but considerest not the beam that is in thine own eye?

4 Or how wilt thou say to thy brother, Let me pull out the mote out of thine eye, and behold a beam is in thine own eye?

5 Thou hypocrite, first cast out the beam out of thine own eye; and then shalt thou see clearly to cast out the mote out of thy brother's eye.

6 Give not that which is holy unto the dogs: neither cast ye your pearls before swine, lest they trample them under their feet, and turn again and rent you.

7 Ask, and it shall be given you; seek, and ye shall find; knock, and it shall be opened unto you.

8 For every one that asketh,

receiveth; and he that seeketh, findeth; and to him that knocketh, it shall be opened.

9 Or what man is there of you, whom if his son ask bread, will he give him a stone?

10 Or if he ask a fish, will he give him a serpent?

11 If ye then being evil, know how to give good gifts unto your children, how much more shall your father which is in heaven, give good things to them that ask him?

12 Therefore all things whatsoever ye would that men should do to you, do ye even so to them; for this is the law and the prophets.

13 Enter ye in at the strait gate, for wide is the gate and broad is the way that leadeth to destruction, and many there be which go in thereat.

14 Because strait is the gate and narrow is the way which leadeth unto life, and few there be that find it.

15 Beware of false prophets, which come to you in sheeps cloathing, but inwardly they are ravening wolves.

16 Ye shall know them by their fruits: Do men gather grapes of thorns, or figs of forth evil fruit, neither can a corrupt tree bring forth good fruit.

19 Every tree that bringeth not forth good fruit, is hewn down and cast into the fire.

20 Wherefore by their fruits ye shall know them.

21 Not every one that saith unto me LORD! LORD! shall enter into the kingdom of heaven: but he that doth the will of my father, which is in heaven.

22 Many will say to me in that day, Lord, Lord, have we not prophesied in thy name? and in thy name have cast out devils, and in thy name done many wonderful works.

23 And then will I profess unto them, I never knew you: Depart from me ye that work iniquity.

24 Therefore whosoever heareth these sayings of mine, and doth them, I will liken him unto a wise man which built his house upon a rock.

25 And the rain descended, and the floods came, and the winds blew, and beat upon that house, and it fell not, for it was founded upon a rock.

26 And every one that

158   CHRIST's Sermon on the Moun

and the floods came, and the winds blew, and beat upon that house; and it fell, and great was the fall of it.

28 And it came to pass, when Jesus had ended these sayings, the peopl nished at his doctr

29 For he taug one having author as the scribes.

Composed by the first general Council, held at the City of Nice, *by* Constantine the Great *(in his Palace) with 318 Bishops from divers Parts.*

I Believe in one God, the Father Almighty Maker of Heaven and Earth, and of all Things visible and invisible. And in one Lord Jesus Christ, the only begotten Son of God, begotten of his Father before all Worlds, God of God, Light of Light, very God of very God, begotten not made, being of one Substance with the Father, by whom all Things were made;--- who for us Men, and for our Salvation, came down from Heaven, and was incarnate by the Holy Ghost, of the Virgin Mary, and was made Man, and was crucified also for us under Pontius Pilate; he suffered and was buried and the third Day rose again, according to the Scriptures, and ascended into Heaven; and sitteth on the right Hand of the Father; and he shall come again with Glory, to judge both the Quick and the Dead, whose Kingdom shall have no End. And I believe in the Holy Ghost, the Lord and Giver of Life, who proceedeth from the Father and the Son, who with the Father and the Son together is worshipped and glorified, who spake by the Prophets. And I believe one Catholick and apostolic Church. I acknowledge one Baptism for the Remission of Sins. And I look for the Resurrection of the Dead; and the Life of the World to come. AMEN.